PANTHER VS A30 CHALLENGER

Operation *Market Garden* 1944

IVO VAN DER SPOEL

OSPREY PUBLISHING
Bloomsbury Publishing Plc
Kemp House, Chawley Park, Cumnor Hill, Oxford OX2 9PH, UK
Bloomsbury Publishing Ireland Limited,
29 Earlsfort Terrace, Dublin 2, D02 AY28, Ireland
Bloomsbury Publishing Inc.
1359 Broadway, 12th Floor, New York, NY 10018, USA
E-mail: info@ospreypublishing.com
www.ospreypublishing.com

First published in Great Britain in 2026

A catalogue record for this book is available from the British Library.

ISBN: PB 9781472874009; eBook 9781472874016;
ePDF 9781472873989; XML 9781472873996

26 27 28 29 30 10 9 8 7 6 5 4 3 2 1

Maps by bounford.com
Index by Mark Swift
Typeset by Lumina Datamatics Ltd
Printed by Repro India Ltd.

MIX
Paper
FSC FSC® C047271

Osprey Publishing supports the Woodland Trust, the UK's leading woodland conservation charity.

To find out more about our authors and books visit **www.ospreypublishing.com**. Here you will find extracts, author interviews, details of forthcoming events and the option to sign up for our newsletter.

For product safety related questions contact productsafety@bloomsbury.com

Dedication
To my parents, for their unceasing support.

Acknowledgements
The author would like to thank the following organizations: TracesOfWar, The Light Dragoons Regimental Association, The Netherlands Institute of Military History, Overloon War Museum, National Military Museum, Freedom Museum, Museum Bunker Alkmaar '40-'45, British Breakout from Normandy Museum, germandocsinrussia.org and panzerworld.com

Title-page photograph: A vigilant crewman watches the sky from the top of his Panther Ausf D. Air attacks became an increasing threat to German armoured formations as the Luftwaffe lost control of the skies. While Allied fighter-bombers struggled to destroy dispersed and concealed tanks, they wreaked havoc on supply columns and assembly areas. (Imwar/Alamy Stock Photo)

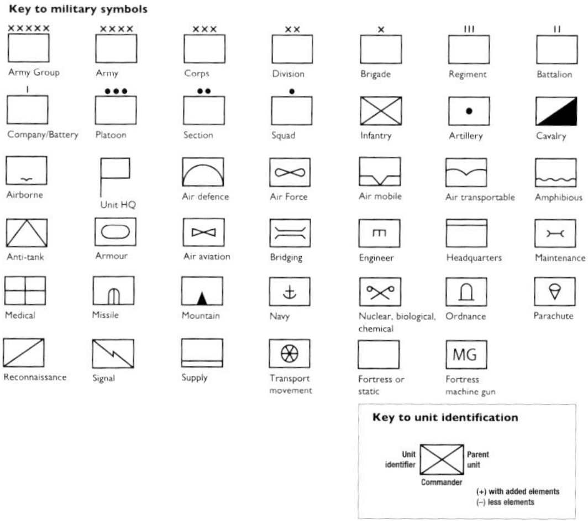

CONTENTS

INTRODUCTION

Operation *Market Garden* entered its fourth day on 20 September 1944. From its inception the ambitious Allied plan hinged on the ability of airborne forces to capture and hold a string of bridges to facilitate a rapid ground offensive into the Netherlands. Ensuring an uninterrupted advance by the ground forces was vital to the success of the operation. Any blown bridge, ambush or roadblock along the route was guaranteed to upset the strict timetable and cause *Market Garden* to spiral out of control. Little interference was expected from Germany's battered armed forces when the operation was launched on 17 September, but by the 20th the energetic counter-attacks of a revitalized Wehrmacht had proved this assumption wrong.

The greatest danger was faced by the British 1st Airborne Division that formed the northern tip of the great 'airborne carpet' and was the furthest behind enemy lines. Its landing west of Arnhem on 17 September was rapidly contained by nearby German forces and only one battalion had made it to the bridge over the Rhine River in downtown Arnhem. By 20 September this beleaguered force had heroically resisted German counter-attacks for days but was fighting on its last reserves of manpower and ammunition. Organized resistance came to an end that night, giving the Germans control of the vital Rhine bridge.

South of Arnhem in the centre of the carpet, the armoured spearhead of the ground advance had reached the US 82d Airborne Division at Nijmegen early on 19 September only to learn that the paratroopers had failed to secure the massive bridge over the Waal River. Bitter fighting through the streets of Nijmegen and a daring river crossing finally captured the bridge by the evening of 20 September, but by then it was too late to reach the beleaguered British at the Arnhem bridge.

At the start of the carpet in the far south the US 101st Airborne Division had been the first to link up with the British ground forces on the evening of 18 September.

Only one Challenger has survived mostly intact, thanks to its post-war adoption by the Royal Netherlands Army. In 1954 it was given to a museum in Delfzijl. Since 1976 this unique Challenger has complemented a Cromwell of 15/19 Hussars and a Panther of Panzer-Brigade 107 in the Overloon War Museum. (Author's Photograph)

The overstretched division had the difficult task of defending the long flanks of the single road to Arnhem that snaked through its sector across numerous small waterways. The vulnerability of the narrow corridor, and dire consequences for Operation *Market Garden* should it be severed, were quickly recognized by German commanders. From the first day of *Market Garden* to its last, this stretch of road was under attack from the flanks, earning it the nickname 'Hell's Highway'. A major clash for the corridor took place on the fateful 20 September when a tank battle raged outside the village of Son, 8km north of Eindhoven, for control of the nearby bridge over the Wilhelmina Canal.

On the German side stood menacing fighting vehicles with a reputation for deadly firepower and impregnable armour. Often regarded as one of the best tanks of World War II, the Panther was designed to give Germany's armoured force a qualitative advantage over the numerical superiority of Allied armour. Since its combat debut in the summer of 1943 the Panther had proved its fighting prowess, but behind the front it troubled German logisticians and mechanics with its high upkeep requirements and persistent reliability issues.

The Panthers that lashed out at the Son bridge were organized along new lines. They were not part of a famed *Panzer-Division*, but of a smaller and independent *Panzer-Brigade* that was intended for quick but deadly counter-thrusts in defence of Germany's crumbling front lines. Hard-hitting but with poor endurance, these brigades combined a small battalion of Panthers with an armoured-infantry battalion riding in heavily armed half-tracks. The attack on Son was a baptism of fire for Panzer-

The only remaining Panther of Panzer-Brigade 107 stands in the Overloon War Museum, located a stone's throw away from the spot where it was knocked out on 12 October 1944. The turret number designates it as a tank of the 2. Kompanie, the unit that spearheaded the first attack on Son on 19 September. (Author's Photograph)

Brigade 107 after it had been formed in a mere six weeks from a core of Eastern Front veterans bolstered by replacements.

Holding 'Hell's Highway' was a force of American airborne infantry and British armour that included a handful of odd and largely forgotten tanks. Often described as an ungainly stopgap, the A30 Challenger was an early attempt by British tank designers to mount the powerful 76.2mm 17-pdr anti-tank gun on the fast Cromwell cruiser tank. The Challenger's development took years and involved the lengthening of the Cromwell hull to fit an oversized turret. Doubt was cast on the Challenger's worth in combat due to its high profile and relatively thin armour, but a modest production run of 200 was nonetheless ordered and by August 1944 it saw action in North-West Europe as a so-called 'hole puncher' in support of the more numerous but under-gunned Cromwell.

At Son the Challenger fought in the ranks of 15/19 Hussars, an armoured reconnaissance regiment that usually served as the vanguard of 11th Armoured Division. After a month-long advance through France and Belgium the battle-hardened regiment had been detached from its parent division and assigned to protect the US 101st Airborne Division in Operation *Market Garden*.

On 20 September a series of sharp engagements took place among windmills, canals and villages that left five Panther tanks knocked out by the guns of 15/19 Hussars. Tank-on-tank combat is largely decided by positioning and situational awareness, not just armour and firepower, and in this regard 15/19 Hussars used its Cromwells and Challengers to great effect. The opposing *Panzer-Brigade* struggled with impassable terrain obstacles and a rushed deployment that put its Panthers at a tactical disadvantage, creating opportunities that 15/19 Hussars skilfully exploited.

This is a history of two rival tanks, of their conceptual origin in the early years of World War II, of their development as armoured fighting vehicles and use as tactical tools, of the crews that served in them and of their clash in combat at a pivotal moment in Operation *Market Garden*.

CHRONOLOGY

1941

22 August Britain's War Office sets a requirement for a 17-pdr-armed tank of British design.

25 November Germany's Heereswaffenamt issues specifications for a new German tank to outclass the Soviet T-34.

1942

9 May Details of the Challenger are announced to the Tank Board.

11 May The MAN proposal for the Panther is chosen.

1943

11 January The first serial Panther is produced.

21 January The first complete Challenger prototype is inspected by War Office representatives and a limited production run of 200 is approved.

5 July Combat debut of the Panther on the Eastern Front.

1944

March Challenger serial production commences.

March The Panther Ausf G replaces the Ausf A. Production peaks in the following months.

6 June Operation *Overlord*. Combat debut of the Cromwell and Sherman Firefly in Normandy.

18 July Panzer-Brigade 107 is established.

3 August Combat debut of the Challenger in Normandy.

19 August Combat debut of 15/19 Hussars in Normandy.

16 September Panzer-Brigade 107 deploys to the Western Front by rail.

17 September Operation *Market Garden* is launched.

18 September British ground forces reach American paratroopers in Eindhoven. Panzer-Brigade 107 arrives in the Netherlands.

19 September 15/19 Hussars comes under command of the US 101st Airborne Division to defend the Eindhoven–Son area. Panzer-Brigade 107 attacks Son in the evening.

20 September Tank battle at Son.

November Panzer-Brigade 107 is absorbed into the revived 25. Panzergrenadier-Division.

1945

March The Cromwells and Challengers of 15/19 Hussars are replaced with the new A34 Comet.

August The last Challenger is produced.

One of the first Challengers is displayed next to a German Tiger I heavy tank at the School of Tank Technology. This Tiger I with turret number 131 was captured by British forces in Tunisia in 1943 and shipped to Britain for further study. The limited width of the Challenger stands out in this side-by-side comparison. (piemags/ww2archive/Alamy Stock Photo)

DESIGN AND DEVELOPMENT

A30 CHALLENGER ORIGINS

While the Challenger experienced a long and tumultuous development characterized by uncertainty over its intended role, the end result can best be described as an up-gunned cruiser tank. As such there are two parts to its origin story. One concerns the evolution of Britain's cruiser tanks and the other the radical leaps in firepower that were necessitated by changing battlefield conditions.

The doctrinal framework for cruiser tanks dated back to World War I and evolved during the interwar period into practical designs by the late 1930s when rearmament began. Cruiser tanks inherited the cavalry's traditional role of rapid exploitation and pursuit that the horse could no longer perform in the face of modern firepower. Like the cavalry, cruiser tanks were to embody mobility, but combine this with armour and firepower that made them a force to be reckoned with as they surged behind enemy lines in great sweeping actions. Above all, cruiser tanks and the armoured divisions of which they were a part were operational tools. Their value lay not in winning tactical battles but in outflanking enemy defences, overrunning headquarters and severing supply lines, thereby causing the entire enemy front to collapse. Creating the conditions for cruiser tanks to rampage into the enemy rear was left to the infantry tanks, which traded mobility in favour of protection so they could batter a way through enemy defences in cooperation with the infantry and artillery, opening a breach for cruiser tanks to

Prime Minister Winston Churchill inspects a Cromwell tank of 2 Welsh Guards, March 1944. The prominent ball mounting for the hull Besa machine gun required the visor plate to be set vertically, significantly reducing its effectiveness compared to the single sloping glacis of the Panther. The hull Besa was omitted on the Challenger, but the vertical visor plate was retained. (Niday Picture Library/Alamy Stock Photo)

surge through. This was the doctrinal foundation of British armoured warfare that split its tank designs into two distinct classes until the post-war advent of the 'capital tank' merged their roles into a single vehicle that could perform both tasks reasonably well.

The basic design of Britain's cruiser tanks remained remarkably consistent throughout the war due to logistical restrictions, doctrinal preferences and a justified fear that radical design changes would delay production and leave Britain with insufficient tanks. From the A13 that saw action in France in 1940 up to the A34 Comet that crossed the Rhine in 1945, British cruiser tanks shared fundamental features. Mobility was their main asset, which required good automotive performance and light weight, while a low profile made them small targets. The Christie suspension, narrow tracks and rear drive were other enduring design characteristics. While it had many upsides, a downside of the Christie suspension was that it occupied space along the sides of the hull, which was particularly unfortunate for British tanks as they were subject to width restrictions imposed by Britain's narrow railway loading gauge. Coupled with a tactical demand for a low profile, this led to British tanks having small dimensions that limited the diameter of their turret ring. As an efficient turret also requires working room for three men, a radio and a coaxial machine gun, this left little free space for the main gun. As British early war doctrine placed great emphasis on firing on the move, tank armament had to be mounted quite deep into the turret to balance its weight and allow the gunner to keep the gun level using a shoulder brace. While this method disappeared as heavier armament was introduced, the demand for a balanced but space-inefficient gun remained.

Many of these restrictions and demands were still in place when the War Office issued the specifications for what would become the Cromwell following the fall of France in May–June 1940. During the brief campaign British cruiser tanks were criticized for their inadequate protection, poor reliability and main armament that would soon be outdated. It was clear that the next cruiser tank needed frontal armour as thick as 75mm and a turret large enough to fit three men and the new 57mm 6-pdr gun.

Ideally, this would have been the moment to assess the state of armoured warfare, learn lessons from the campaign in France and take the time to develop a future-proof tank, but the situation was far from ideal. Britain's best tanks were lost in France, more were desperately needed in North Africa and the homeland was under threat of invasion. Under these dire circumstances it was decided that priority should be given to mass producing flawed but existing tank designs while the next generation would be based on readily available technology. Nuffield Mechanization & Aero was chosen to develop a new cruiser tank as its design was largely based on the already existing A15 Crusader and therefore most likely to enter production quickly. It also meant that the Cromwell, as it became known, would be shackled to many of the design restrictions that had held back British tanks, including the inability to be up-gunned easily due to a narrow turret ring.

Lack of space could drastically shorten a tank's service life because the arms race between firepower and protection demanded ever-larger guns to remain competitive. At the same time, combat experience shifted the focus of tank armament in new directions. British tanks originally carried a main gun that was optimized for punching through armour above all else. The 40mm 2-pdr fired a solid armour-piercing (AP) shot that was very potent against enemy tanks but had little utility against unarmoured targets such as lorries and anti-tank guns. Against such targets a high-explosive (HE) shell that burst on impact into a spray of splinters was much more effective, but these were sorely lacking in British tanks, which had to rely on their short-range machine guns to deal with unarmoured targets. A small number of close-support tanks with large-calibre howitzers were allotted to armoured formations, but their intended role was primarily smoke laying.

The emphasis on armour-piercing performance continued with Britain's next gun, the 6-pdr, which was capable against tanks but lacked an effective HE shell. It was not until 1942 that the arrival of new American medium tanks mounting 75mm dual-purpose guns gave British tank crews a weapon capable of firing potent HE shells. Demand for a dual-purpose weapon increased to the point that a similar 75mm gun, based on a modified 6-pdr, became the standard armament for British tanks, including the Cromwell. What was gained in explosive firepower was unfortunately lost in armour-piercing potential, however, as the 75mm gun was weaker than the 6-pdr in this regard due to its lower velocity. While this was not a pressing issue as long as the Germans were fielding the PzKpfw III and PzKpfw IV medium tanks, it was anticipated that they would introduce more heavily armoured tanks that the 75mm would struggle to penetrate. To ensure that British armoured formations had the means to fight back against these potential adversaries it was decided to equip a portion of cruiser tanks with the most powerful armour-piercing weapon that was available, even if putting it in a tank would prove to be a challenge.

A30 CHALLENGER DEVELOPMENT

The Challenger's development consisted of two phases. From August 1941 to January 1943 the vehicle was in its prototype stage and the primary concern was to modify the Cromwell quickly into a stopgap solution capable of carrying the 17-pdr gun. This stage came to an end on 21 January 1943 when the first complete prototype was evaluated by War Office representatives, who considered it a functional and necessary stopgap but not much more and the total production run was limited to just 200 vehicles. From this moment to the Challenger's baptism of fire in August 1944 the second stage of its development was directed at refining the prototypes into machines worthy of entering serial production and front-line service. Failed trials led to redesigns and the delays caused the Challenger to miss Operation *Overlord*. When the first batch of Challengers finally saw action in August 1944 it concluded a three-year development process from theoretical concept to an actual fighting machine. Substantial improvements continued to be implemented during production and it was not until August 1945 that the last of the 200 Challengers rolled off the assembly line.

Turning back the clock to August 1941, it was at this early stage in the conflict that the War Office first recognized the need for some sort of fighting vehicle capable of carrying the 17-pdr gun. That such a powerful weapon was already a consideration was thanks to the forward thinking of the Royal Artillery regarding heavy anti-tank guns since late 1940. Unfortunately British tank design, due to the aforementioned restrictions, had lagged behind gun development and no armoured vehicle was available that could accommodate the 17-pdr gun in a fully rotating turret.

The best candidate at the time was the new Cromwell cruiser tank. Unfortunately, the initial Nuffield design, known as the A24 Cavalier, was shaping up to be a thoroughly mediocre tank that used an underpowered 410hp (306kW) Liberty engine and inherited the poor reliability of the Crusader upon which it was based. Thankfully, a parallel design had been initiated by the Birmingham Railway Carriage & Wagon Company (BRC&W) with the help of Rolls-Royce that sought to improve the automotive performance of the struggling Cavalier. By modifying the powerful Merlin aircraft engine into the 600hp (447kW) Meteor tank engine, installing the modern Merritt-Brown gearbox, redesigning the radiator and strengthening the Christie suspension, the fast and reliable A27M Cromwell was created that would see action

The lengthened hull of the Challenger was supported by a sixth set of road wheels. The toothed sprocket that drives the track can be seen at the rear while the small idler wheel is positioned at the front of the hull. This factory-fresh Challenger still has its thin metal track guards intact. (piemags/archive/military/Alamy Stock Photo)

in 1944; but a limiting factor of the Cromwell that could not be easily improved was the narrow turret ring that restricted the main armament to a 6-pdr or the similarly sized 75mm gun. To satisfy the War Office demand for a British tank carrying the 17-pdr gun in a fully rotating turret, the Rolls-Royce and BRC&W team began modifying the Cromwell in early 1942 to create the Challenger.

As the Challenger would be the first, and for a long time the only, British tank mounting the 17-pdr gun it was vital to get the tank into production quickly. Existing components had to be used wherever possible, even if they made a poor match. The Mk II version of the 17-pdr was only a minor modification of the original field gun and demanded a wasteful amount of space. The only turret capable of mounting the gun was based on the TOG II heavy tank prototype. While the TOG II's turret had room for the gun, four men and ammunition, it was also tall and not as well armoured as the turret on the Cromwell. It used a peculiar ball pivot mechanism on the hull floor to support its weight and incorporated a bulky electrical traverse system. The turret demanded a 70in (178cm) turret ring but the Cromwell was limited to 60in (152cm), so it was decided to enlarge the fighting compartment by widening it over the tracks and lengthening it through the inclusion of an additional pair of road wheel stations. This resulted in a raised platform called the 'turret box' that could fit the required turret ring. The added weight risked overloading the suspension, however, so the hull side armour thickness was reduced by half. This decision, coupled with the thinner turret armour, would haunt the Challenger for the rest of its service life.

The issue concerning the Challenger's perceived lack of protection came to a head on 21 January 1943 when a War Office advisory committee inspected the first complete prototype to judge if it was worth a production run of 200 vehicles. Spurred on by the Chief Instructor of the Gunnery Wing at the AFV School, Lieutenant-Colonel W.B. Turner, the discussion honed in on the tactical utility of the Challenger. By this time the lessons from North Africa on the importance of dual-purpose guns had been embraced by the AFV School and Turner was sceptical about a tank designed

A Challenger demonstrates its improved idler wheel. The open-spoke design, coupled with a mud scraper, prevented dirt from clogging the wheel and throwing off the track. This malfunction was most likely to occur when steering in reverse on muddy slopes, a common manoeuvre in combat for moving out of a 'hull down' firing position. (Tank Museum TM 8202-D5)

Challenger T271926, viewed here from the rear, served as a test vehicle for improvements to the armoured protection and related strengthening of the chassis. The two small boxes on either side of the towing hook contain smoke generators that can be electrically ignited by the driver to create defensive 'tail smoke' behind the vehicle. (Tank Museum TM 11536-016)

solely to fight other tanks, especially if it had to do so with reduced armour. Turner characterized the Challenger as a costly but useless 'white elephant' that offered only a limited advantage at extreme ranges where its poor protection was less of a liability. While this criticism effectively ended any hope of mass production, the committee did endorse the limited production of 200 Challengers as a stopgap solution to satisfy the General Staff policy that a proportion of cruiser tanks should carry the 17-pdr gun. As it was deemed unlikely that the Challenger could be up-armoured to an acceptable standard, the conclusion of the committee spurred the development of alternatives that would result in the Comet and Sherman Firefly.

Even an emergency stopgap still had to be accepted for active service so throughout 1943 and early 1944 the Challenger prototypes were subjected to numerous trials before serial production could commence. Experience in North Africa had shown the vital importance of durability, so the Challenger had to pass a gruelling 3,000-mile (4,828km) course that revealed problems with the overloaded suspension. Gunnery trials were mostly positive, the fast and precise electrical turret traverse system proving excellent once the initial issues were fixed. Being on the receiving end of a gunnery trial was less positive as the immunity test revealed unacceptable weaknesses in the front turret armour. Patching up these weak spots pushed the start of production into 1944 and it became increasingly unlikely that the Challenger would be available in time for Operation *Overlord*. Serial production finally commenced in March 1944 but delays prevented the build-up of sufficient numbers of Challengers for front-line use until early August.

Modifications were implemented on the production line and in the field. The much-criticized lack of protection was improved by introducing a thicker turret nose plate starting with the 41st Challenger and the last 100 Challengers had additional armour welded to their frontal surfaces. This improvement had been in development since September 1943 and included the strengthening of the suspension to deal with the additional weight. The up-armoured Challenger boasted frontal protection comparable to that of the new Comet while its 17-pdr gun was a more potent armour-piercing weapon than the Comet's 77mm gun.

A serious defect revealed itself in the muddy fields of Western Europe where the Challenger's front idler wheel had a tendency to collect mud when reversing. In some cases this resulted in the shedding of the track and damage to the idler wheel. The malfunction was severe enough to warrant a withdrawal of all Challengers from front-line service in late 1944 pending the introduction of a solution, although not all units appear to have complied with the order. An improved idler with mud scraper fixed the problem and became a standard modification starting in January 1945, but the issue blotted the otherwise excellent reputation for reliability that the Challenger shared with the Cromwell and Comet. In the end, the Challenger only appeared in small numbers and could never escape its reputation as an ungainly stopgap, but those who fought in it valued its excellent combination of firepower and mobility.

Dimensions (l×w×h): 8.03m×2.91m×2.67m

Firepower
Main gun: Ordnance, Q.F., 17-pdr, Mk II (76.2×584mmR)
Ammunition capacity: 48
Machine gun: Browning M1919A4 (7.62×63mm)
Ammunition capacity: 15 belts of 250 rounds (3,750 total)
Cyclic rate of fire: 550rd/min
Launcher: Bombthrower 2in (51mm)
Ammunition capacity: 30
Turret ring diameter: 178cm
Elevation: -10 to +20 degrees
Maximum traverse speed: 30 degrees per second at 2,700rpm

Communications
Crew: 5
Radio: Wireless Set No. 19 Mk III
Intercom: 4 connections
A-Set voice range: 16km
B-Set voice range: 900m

Armour (degrees from vertical)
Turret nose: 63/102mm*@6°
Turret front side: 63/88mm*@0°
Turret side: 40mm@0°
Hull visor: 64/89mm*@0°
Hull glacis: 30mm@70°
Hull nose: 57/82mm*@20°
Hull side upper: 51mm@0°
Hull side lower: 14+14mm@0°
* Original/upgraded

Automotive
Combat weight: 33 tonnes (34.5 tonnes with all additional armour)
Engine: Rolls-Royce Meteor
Power: 600hp (447kW) at 2,550rpm
Power to weight: 18hp (13.5kW) per tonne
Gearbox: Merritt-Brown Z.5 (5 forward gears, 1 reverse)
Fuel capacity: 527l (petrol)

Mobility
Maximum on-road speed: 51km/h
Average off-road speed: 28km/h
Maximum reverse speed: 3km/h
Range on-road: 240km
Range off-road: 110km
Ground clearance: 41cm
Length of track on ground: 450cm
Track width: 39cm
Ground pressure: 0.93kg/cm^2
Climb: 30 degrees
Trench crossing: 259cm
Fording: 122cm
Step climbing: 91cm

A30 CHALLENGER

Challenger T271940 departed from Birmingham spick-and-span with a fresh coat of paint. In front-line service with 3 Tp, B Sqn, 15/19 Hussars, its flimsy track guards were torn off and layers of French, Belgian and Dutch mud clung to its armour. Only the most essential tactical markings were applied by 15/19 Hussars. A number ranging from one to four identified the troop, surrounded by a triangle, square or circle for A, B or C Sqn respectively. These markings were painted in white to identify the unit as a divisional armoured reconnaissance regiment.

PANTHER ORIGINS

The Challenger may have been late to the action, but its design was initiated with considerable foresight at a point in the war when heavier German tanks had not yet made an appearance. This gave the Challenger the benefit of a long development period that resulted in a mature design, even if some features were no longer cutting-edge by the time it saw action. By contrast the Panther was hastily designed and prematurely forced into mass production after Germany was caught off-guard by the sudden appearance of a superior enemy tank on the battlefield.

This shock came in the form of the T-34 medium tank that was encountered following the German invasion of the Soviet Union in the summer of 1941. Facing a thickly armoured opponent was nothing new for veteran German tankers, but where the Soviet T-34 differed from the sluggish heavy tanks that had been defeated in France the previous year was that it combined a sophisticated armour layout of sharply angled plates with superior off-road mobility and deadly firepower in a medium-weight package that was well-suited for mass production by Soviet industry.

In November 1941 a special commission of officers from the Heereswaffenamt (Army Ordnance Department) and designers from Germany's leading arms manufacturers visited the Eastern Front to assess the dire tank situation. The sloped armour and wide tracks of a captured T-34 made an impression on the designers and experienced German commanders, represented by Generaloberst Heinz Guderian, stressed the need for heavier tank armament capable of decisively knocking-out the T-34 at long range.

Up-gunning existing designs was fairly easy but only offered a short-term solution. The best tanks that Germany had invaded the Soviet Union with were the PzKpfw III and PzKpfw IV. Both dated from the middle of the 1930s and were the first proper battle tanks that resulted from German rearmament. They were similar to British cruiser tanks of the time as they prioritized mobility over protection and were concentrated in dedicated armoured divisions that were intended for decisive manoeuvres at the operational level. In terms of armament the PzKpfw III resembled a standard cruiser tank with a small-calibre anti-tank gun while the PzKpfw IV functioned similarly to a specialist close-support tank mounting a large-calibre howitzer. An advantage over contemporary British designs was that the larger dimensions of the Panzers gave them the ability to mount heavier guns than they were originally designed for without requiring major alterations to the hull or turret. The PzKpfw IV had the most room to spare and could be up-gunned with a high-velocity 75mm gun capable of defeating the T-34. The smaller PzKpfw III had already swapped its original 37mm gun for a 50mm gun by 1941, but confidently facing a T-34 required the same high-velocity 75mm gun that the PzKpfw IV was carrying and this was too much for the PzKpfw III turret. While the improved PzKpfw IV would soldier on for the rest of the war as a capable battle tank, the PzKpfw III chassis was relegated to the infantry-support role as a turretless *Sturmgeschütz* (assault gun) that mounted the high-velocity 75mm gun in a fixed superstructure with limited traverse.

Achieving mere parity with the T-34 would not suffice for the long-term, however. A completely new tank had to be introduced to regain a technological advantage.

The commander's cupola of the Panther Ausf D was constructed in a simple drum shape with six direct-vision blocks that had large gaps between them. The cupola was replaced by a better cast design on the Ausf A and Ausf G that featured seven periscopes for improved all-round vision and protection. (michael cremin/ Alamy Stock Photo)

Design work on a successor to both the PzKpfw III and PzKpfw IV had been ongoing for some years but was mainly focused on improving mobility while staying within a 20-tonne weight class that did not allow for a major increase in protection or firepower. Some within the Heereswaffenamt nevertheless advocated its introduction on the grounds that it would be quick to design, cheap to produce and could make use of existing military infrastructure – a similar line of reasoning to that dictating British tank procurement at the time. The German political leadership did not agree with this view, however, and demanded a greater leap in fighting power than a 20-tonne tank could offer. Only a completely new design of 30 tonnes, incorporating the latest technology based on combat experience, would fulfil the demands of German tankers and secure a technological advantage over their opponents for years to come.

PANTHER DEVELOPMENT

The development of the Panther began mere days after the commission's return from the Eastern Front. On 25 November 1941 the Heereswaffenamt contracted Daimler-Benz and Maschinenfabrik Augsburg-Nürnberg (MAN) to compete in the design for a new tank designated the VK 30.02. In the meantime Maybach, Germany's tank engine specialist, commenced work on a 700PS (515kW) engine that was to be as small and lightweight as possible. Rheinmetall-Borsig developed an even more powerful 75mm high-velocity gun and a turret large enough to accommodate three crewmen. After five months of frantic work Daimler-Benz and MAN presented their competing designs for the VK 30.02, by now known as the Panther, to a special advisory commission in May 1942.

The Daimler-Benz proposal made a strong first impression due to its close resemblance to the T-34, including a space-efficient rear drive that gave it a lower profile compared to the MAN design. Where it fell critically short was in the diameter of its turret ring as this was 50mm too narrow to fit the Rheinmetall turret. In a dilemma that would have been all too familiar to British tank designers, the troubles for Daimler-Benz began with the suspension and its impact on the width of the vehicle. A generous maximum width of 3.2m was allowed, but Daimler-Benz cut into this space by using a simple leaf-spring suspension. Like the Christie type used on British cruiser tanks and the T-34, this suspension took up valuable space on the sides of the hull. The MAN design used an innovative torsion-bar suspension that not only offered superior off-road performance but also occupied less space on the sides of the vehicle. This gave the MAN design wider tracks and better ground pressure, a wider hull with more internal space and crucially a turret ring that could fit the Rheinmetall turret. Daimler-Benz designed a custom turret but this required modifications to the gun and would not be ready in time for mass production. This made MAN the clear winner and its design was unanimously chosen by the commission on 11 May 1942.

The MAN design did come with downsides that would have to be accepted if it were to enter mass production by the end of the year. Its high profile of 2.85m was a consequence of the torsion-bar suspension and front drive. The Daimler-Benz rear drive was one of the most appealing features of its design as it moved the bulky gearbox away from the front of the vehicle and into the rear next to the engine, saving

This burned-out Panther Ausf A has been stripped of all but one of its *Schürzen* plates, revealing the characteristic kink in the rear portion of the upper hull side. This was straightened on the later Ausf G to simplify production. (Imwar/Alamy Stock Photo)

A batch of Panther Ausf G tanks has rolled off the MAN assembly line in Nuremberg and is awaiting transportation. Some foliage has already been applied as camouflage in the hope of hiding them from Allied aircraft on their way to the front. (Imwar/Alamy Stock Photo)

space around the driver's position and avoiding the need for a drive shaft through the fighting compartment. Weight was another serious issue. The Panther proposals had grown to 35 tonnes when they were presented in May 1942. Hitler agreed with the commission's preference for the MAN design but demanded an increase in frontal armour from the specified 60mm to 80mm and by the time the Panther entered mass production its weight had increased to 45 tonnes. The powerful Maybach HL 210 P 30 engine still provided enough power to make it a mobile tank, but the strain on components that had originally been intended for a lighter vehicle would cause persistent reliability issues.

Despite the great rush to get the Panther into the field, it was not until January 1943 that serial production finally commenced. The first Panther variant, confusingly called the Ausf D, suffered from poor manufacture on hastily established production lines and incorporated numerous untested components with unacceptable failure rates. Despite these clear issues, production continued unabated throughout early 1943 to create a Panther force large enough to have an impact on the impending summer offensive on the Eastern Front. As late as June 1943, however, Guderian, by then the *Generalinspekteur der Panzertruppen* (Inspector General of Armoured Troops), was pessimistic about the worth of the Panther. Hundreds had been produced in such a poor state that they had to be painstakingly and repeatedly overhauled to fix a myriad of defects.

The Panther would make its combat debut in the summer offensive whether it was ready or not. A special brigade with 192 Panthers took part in the attack on the Kursk salient on 5 July 1943 and quickly found its strength reduced to just 40 operational tanks by the end of the first day. Mechanical breakdowns took their toll, but tactical mistakes due to insufficient training in the new tanks also led to unnecessary losses. A lack of recovery vehicles caused many immobilized Panthers to be destroyed by their own crews. Nevertheless, some were captured intact, giving

This abandoned Panther Ausf G features many minor modifications, most notably the improved mantlet that was redesigned to prevent armour-piercing shots from ricocheting into the thin hull roof if they struck the lower curve. The new mantlet was introduced in September 1944 but never fully replaced the older type, which remained in production. (NARA)

the Allies valuable insight into the strengths and weaknesses of Germany's latest tank. Combat at Kursk also highlighted the Panther's strong points. Its powerful 75mm gun destroyed T-34s with ease out to extreme ranges while the thick frontal armour successfully resisted Soviet guns up close. On the other hand, exposing the Panther's vulnerable flanks was a fatal mistake due to the combination of thin side armour, exposed ammunition in the fighting compartment and poor escape facilities.

Despite the bad first impression at Kursk the fundamental design of the Panther was considered sound and worthy of further development. In August 1943 a number of improvements were implemented on the 851st Panther that rolled off the production line. This new variant was confusingly designated as the Ausf A, perhaps to signal a fresh start after the Ausf D proved to be more of a prototype than a finished machine. The biggest improvements were made to the turret which was now traversed by a more powerful hydraulic system driven by a power take-off from the engine drive shaft. Unlike the slow system of the Ausf D, the new Ausf A could traverse its turret at higher rates depending on the engine speed. Another major improvement to the turret was the new commander's cupola that incorporated seven periscopes for enhanced all-round vision when closed down. Additional modifications were introduced on the Ausf A as the design matured, including a new ball mount for the hull machine gun and an improved monocular gunsight with two magnification settings. Reliability continued to be a major cause for concern. The improved Maybach HL 230 P30 engine had been introduced during the production run of the Ausf D but suffered from overheating and poor durability. In November 1943 it was governed from 3,000rpm to 2,500rpm in an effort to prolong its lifespan.

In March 1944 the final major modification, the Ausf G, was introduced. By this time the production of Panthers was carried out with greater efficiency and the Ausf G was mainly intended to streamline the design further. Considerable time and effort had already been spent on simplifying the hull layout for the 'Panther II' project.

OPPOSITE

The Panther's final drive was not only prone to failure, but also difficult to access. Parts of the driver's compartment had to be disassembled and the transmission lifted out through an opening in the hull roof using a crane. Frequent breakdowns, insufficient spare parts and overworked mechanics kept many Panther-equipped units chronically understrength. (Imwar/Alamy Stock Photo)

This planned successor was conceived in early 1943 as a way to increase armour thickness beyond the capabilities of the original Panther and to standardize certain components with the Tiger II heavy tank. The Panther II project was not pursued further but the streamlined hull layout was implemented on the Ausf G. By adjusting the thickness and angle of certain plates, sufficient internal space was gained to allow for three more rounds to be carried without increasing the overall weight of the tank. Production was also simplified by the standardization of plate thicknesses, which helped the Ausf G to become the most-produced Panther variant.

While numerous, the Panther Ausf G was also the hardest hit by being on the losing side of a total war. In the summer of 1944 Germany suffered crushing defeats in the east and west while its industry was under sustained aerial bombardment and critical resources such as fuel were running out. Panthers left the factory increasingly barren as rubber and even paint were in short supply. Crew training became rudimentary and tactical competence dropped while Allied tank numbers and crew experience increased. The Panther remained a capable tank to the end but like all equipment it was only as good as the logistical system that supported it.

Dimensions (l×w×h): 8.66m×3.42m×2.85m

Firepower

Main gun: 7.5cm Kampfwagenkanone 42 L/70 (75×640mmR)
Ammunition capacity: 82
Machine guns: 3× MG 34 (7.92×57mm)
Ammunition capacity: 32 belts of 150 rounds (4,800 total)
Cyclic rate of fire: 900rd/min
Launcher: *Nahverteidigungswaffe* (91mm)
Ammunition capacity: 12
Turret ring diameter: 165cm
Elevation: -8 to +18 degrees
Maximum traverse speed: 20 degrees per second at 2,500rpm

Communications

Crew: 5
Radio: Fu 5
Intercom: 4 connections
Wireless voice range: 3km

Armour (degrees from vertical)

Mantlet: 100mm (curved)
Turret front: 100mm@12°
Turret side: 45mm@25°
Hull glacis: 80mm@55°
Hull nose: 50mm@55°
Hull side upper: 50mm@30°
Hull side lower: 40+5mm*@0°
* *Schürzen* side armour

Automotive

Combat weight: 45 tonnes
Engine: Maybach HL 230 P30
Power: 600PS (441kW) at 2,500rpm
Power to weight: 13.3PS (9.8kW) per tonne
Gearbox: AK 7-200 (7 forward gears, 1 reverse)
Fuel capacity: 720l (petrol)

Mobility

Maximum on-road speed: 46km/h
Average off-road speed: 30km/h
Maximum reverse speed: 3km/h
Range on-road: 200km
Range off-road: 100km
Ground clearance: 54cm
Length of track on ground: 392cm
Track width: 66cm
Ground pressure: 0.87kg/cm²
Climb: 30 degrees
Trench crossing: 245cm
Fording: 170cm
Step climbing: 90cm

PANTHER AUSF G

The Panthers of Panzer-Brigade 107 were some of the last to roll off the production lines with *Zimmerit* before this anti-magnetic coating was discontinued in September 1944. Camouflaging the tanks was the responsibility of the unit that fielded them and usually took the form of a three-colour paint scheme. Some Panthers of Panzer-Brigade 107 featured a second *Balkenkreuz* on their turrets. This was likely added in a hurry after the first cross accidentally overlapped with the turret number. This number identified the tank's company, platoon and place within the platoon.

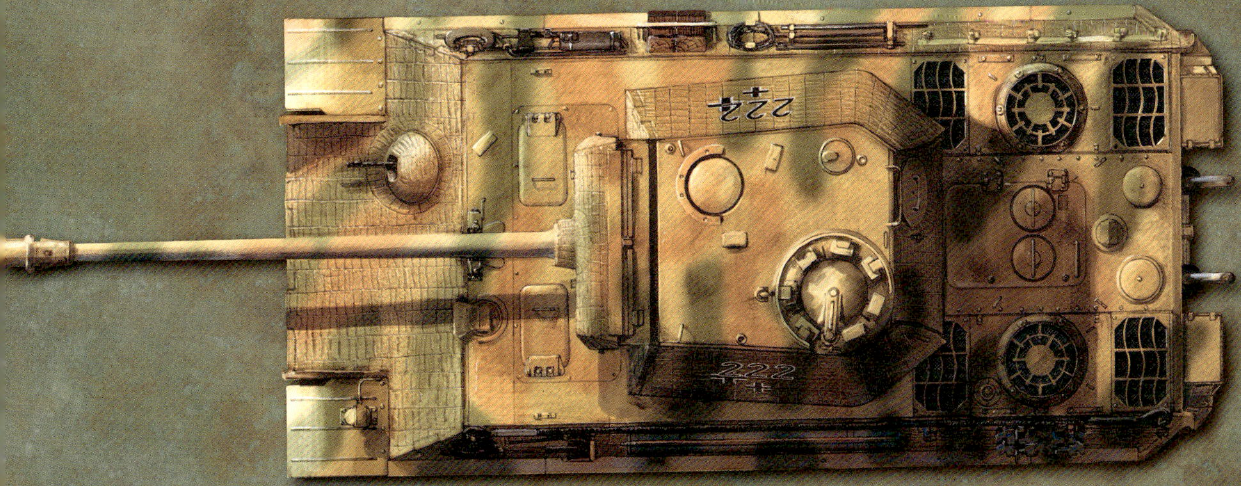

TECHNICAL SPECIFICATIONS

MOBILITY AND RELIABILITY

Despite its heavy armament the Challenger retained the excellent mobility that was expected of a British cruiser tank thanks to its good automotive components. The additional weight reduced its top speed on roads somewhat compared to the lighter Cromwell, but the Challenger had slightly better cross-country performance thanks to its additional pair of road wheels and lengthened tracks. Ground pressure remained high due to the narrow tracks and the Challenger was at risk of bogging in soft ground. The Christie suspension, originally designed for very light tanks, was reaching the limits of what it could comfortably support.

The Panther was also designed with mobility in mind but with a greater emphasis on cross-country performance necessitated by the muddy conditions on the Eastern Front. The wide tracks and interleaved road wheels gave the Panther a very low ground pressure for a tank of its weight while the smooth torsion-bar suspension allowed it to maintain a high speed over rough ground. Despite weighing as much as some heavy tanks, the Panther was propelled by its powerful Maybach engine to a 46km/h top speed that put it on a par with many medium tanks of its time but behind Britain's cruiser tanks.

Where the Panther fell critically short was in the durability of certain key components that led to frequent breakdowns. Its Achilles heel was the overburdened drivetrain that transferred power from the rear engine to the front drive sprockets.

A Panther demonstrates its step-climbing ability. Two spare road wheels are carried on the rear of the turret. Mounting track links and road wheels on the turret was not officially authorized, but was commonly done by units in the field and even, as shown here, by demonstration vehicles at testing facilities. (Associated Press/Alamy Stock Photo)

The sloped armour reduced the available space for the front drive while the increased weight caused by the last-minute demand for a thicker glacis plate could not be taken into account when the parts of the drivetrain were hastily designed. Only sophisticated gearing could handle the stresses put on it by such weight, but Germany lacked the facilities to mass-produce these; nor did it have the high-quality steel that could give simpler gears a longer lifespan. The predictable result was a delicate drivetrain with a short service life, the final drive in particular being prone to failure after just 150km.

A satisfactory solution could not be found and it was up to the drivers to handle their vehicles with care. This was not made easy as the Panther's manual gearbox and single-radius steering were deliberate simplifications for mass production compared to the sophisticated system on the Tiger. Poor shifting or heavy-handed steering, especially on inclines and muddy ground, could quickly reduce a Panther's lifespan in the hands of an inexperienced driver. These shortcomings were increasingly common as fuel shortages reduced training opportunities.

Breakdowns and battle damage overburdened repair facilities that were already struggling with shortages of spare parts. The inaccessibility of some of the Panther's components such as the torsion bars and final drives only increased the repair facilities' workload and led to a pile-up of Panthers awaiting attention, further reducing the availability of the already scarce tank.

British tanks had also suffered from reliability issues at the start of the war because they were rushed into service out of desperation similarly to the Panther. Operations in North Africa showed that broken tanks caused more trouble than they were worth and reliability was set as the top priority for future designs. Neither the Cromwell nor the Challenger would be accepted for years as their issues were worked out through rigorous testing, but when they finally saw action in 1944, they were reliable machines capable of travelling great distances with minimal breakdowns.

FIREPOWER VS ARMOUR

Armour-piercing firepower was a design priority for both the Panther and Challenger. The Panther's Kampfwagenkanone (KwK) 42 high-velocity gun was capable of penetrating most Allied tanks within practical combat range using its standard AP ammunition. Against heavily armoured tanks the Panzergranate 40/42 round offered increased penetration through the use of a tungsten-carbide core instead of explosive filler, but the scarcity of tungsten meant that this ammunition type only saw limited use and generally was not needed to deal with the majority of Allied tanks.

The Challenger was never intended to stand up to such firepower. The thickest plate it inherited from the Cromwell was the 64mm visor plate on the front hull. This was set vertically to facilitate a Besa machine gun on the Cromwell, but this weapon and its operator were removed on the Challenger to make room for more 17-pdr ammunition. Vertical plates offer less protection than angled armour and many British tankers would have preferred a single sloped glacis plate as was the case on the Panther. The Challenger's tall turret only offered 63mm protection at best and spoiled the otherwise low profile of the hull. Attempts were made to increase the Challenger's protection, first by thickening the turret nose plate to 102mm and later by welding additional 25mm plates to the front, but this still was not enough to protect reliably against a gun as powerful as the Panther's KwK 42.

Not getting hit was the best form of protection and in this regard the Challenger mainly had to rely on camouflage to obscure its distinctive turret profile. Attempts were also made to camouflage part of the 17-pdr gun to make it appear shorter, but the tall turret still gave the Challenger away as a priority target among a troop of Cromwells. A good 10 degrees of gun depression allowed the Challenger to use the terrain as cover by occupying 'hull down' positions that kept the majority of the vehicle safely behind a slope and only exposed the gun and a small part of the turret to fire over the crest. In an emergency the Challenger's gunner could fire smoke bombs from a roof-mounted launcher to create a protective smokescreen in the direction that the turret was facing. The driver could activate smoke generators on the rear of the hull to conceal a retreat. These techniques, coupled with the Challenger's good mobility, did more to protect it on the battlefield than its armour.

Knocking out a Panther before it could retaliate was the safest way to deal with one, but its thick frontal armour was a tough nut to crack for even the heaviest Allied guns. The majority of the Panther's front was protected by the 80mm-thick glacis plate set at an angle of 55 degrees. When British experts first examined this plate on a captured Panther, the combination of thickness and slope made them doubt if the 17-pdr gun was powerful enough to pierce it with standard ammunition. Putting the glacis plate to the test in a firing trial revealed that it was more brittle than anticipated due to Germany's dwindling alloy supply. German industry had introduced new production techniques to compensate for the poor metallurgical quality of its steel, but these methods were difficult to apply consistently to a plate as large as the Panther's glacis. Coupled with poor quality control in bombed factories this led to increasing numbers of Panthers rolling off the production lines with flawed glacis plates that could be vulnerable to the

This veteran Challenger of B Sqn's 3 Tp was demonstrated to military photographers in October 1944 when 15/19 Hussars fought in the area around Overloon. The crew has tied a clog to the 'turret protection strip' that shields the gap between the turret and hull, perhaps as a good-luck charm. (Tank Museum 1794-B6)

17-pdr gun depending on range, impact angle and ammunition. Even a partial penetration could transfer enough force to crack the brittle glacis, however, propelling deadly splinters into the interior and weakening the plate, leaving it vulnerable to a follow-up hit.

The other plates that covered the Panther's front were less metallurgically flawed but had other weaknesses. The hull nose plate shielded the lower portion between the tracks and despite being angled at 55 degrees its thickness of just 50mm could not stand up to the 17-pdr gun at short range. The turret was mostly covered by a curved mantlet that presented an awkward target. If struck perfectly in the centre the 100mm of cast armour could be easily penetrated by the 17-pdr, but only a slight deviation would cause the shot to strike the curve and ricochet. This was a good design for the upper part of the mantlet, but its lower half was prone to bouncing projectiles into the thin hull roof armour. This 'shot trap' gave weaker guns like the 75mm of the Cromwell a small chance to disable a Panther frontally so a modification that straightened the lower part of the mantlet was eventually introduced. The turret in general was an unsatisfactory design and by late 1944 the greatly improved *Schmalturm* (narrow turret) was developed but did not enter production. The side armour of the

The Panther did not originally come with *Schürzen* side skirts. These thin metal plates were belatedly introduced in April 1943 to protect the 40mm-thick lower-hull side armour against Soviet anti-tank rifles, which had a chance of penetrating the armour if fired directly side-on at close range. (michael cremin/Alamy Stock Photo)

Panther was comparatively thin and not as angled as the front which made the flanks vulnerable to most Allied guns out to long range.

The 17-pdr gun could get a significant boost in penetrating power if it fired Armour Piercing Discarding Sabot (APDS) rounds. This novel ammunition type propelled a sub-calibre tungsten-carbide projectile using a lightweight casing (the 'sabot') that discarded upon exiting the confines of the barrel, leaving the small 3.6kg projectile to fly off at a very high muzzle velocity of 1,204m/sec with a maximum theoretical armour penetration of 275mm at 100m. In practice APDS was less impressive as the ammunition was still experimental and suffered from teething troubles. The first batch was shipped to Normandy in August 1944 but revealed severe accuracy issues that held it back from widespread service. It was not until late March 1945 that a unit equipped with Challengers mentioned using APDS in combat but missing their target due to confusion over which type of round was loaded. The Challenger's training pamphlet from May 1945 still regarded APDS as speciality ammunition that should only be used at short range when penetration with the regular Armour Piercing Capped Ballistic Capped (APCBC) round was impossible.

Projectile	Muzzle velocity	Projectile weight	100m	500m	1,000m
Pzgr 39/42	935m/sec	6.8kg	185mm*	168mm*	149mm*
APCBC/T Mk 8	884m/sec	7.7kg	174mm*	163mm*	150mm*

*Theoretical penetration of rolled homogeneous armour at 0 degrees.

A30 CHALLENGER AND PANTHER AMMUNITION

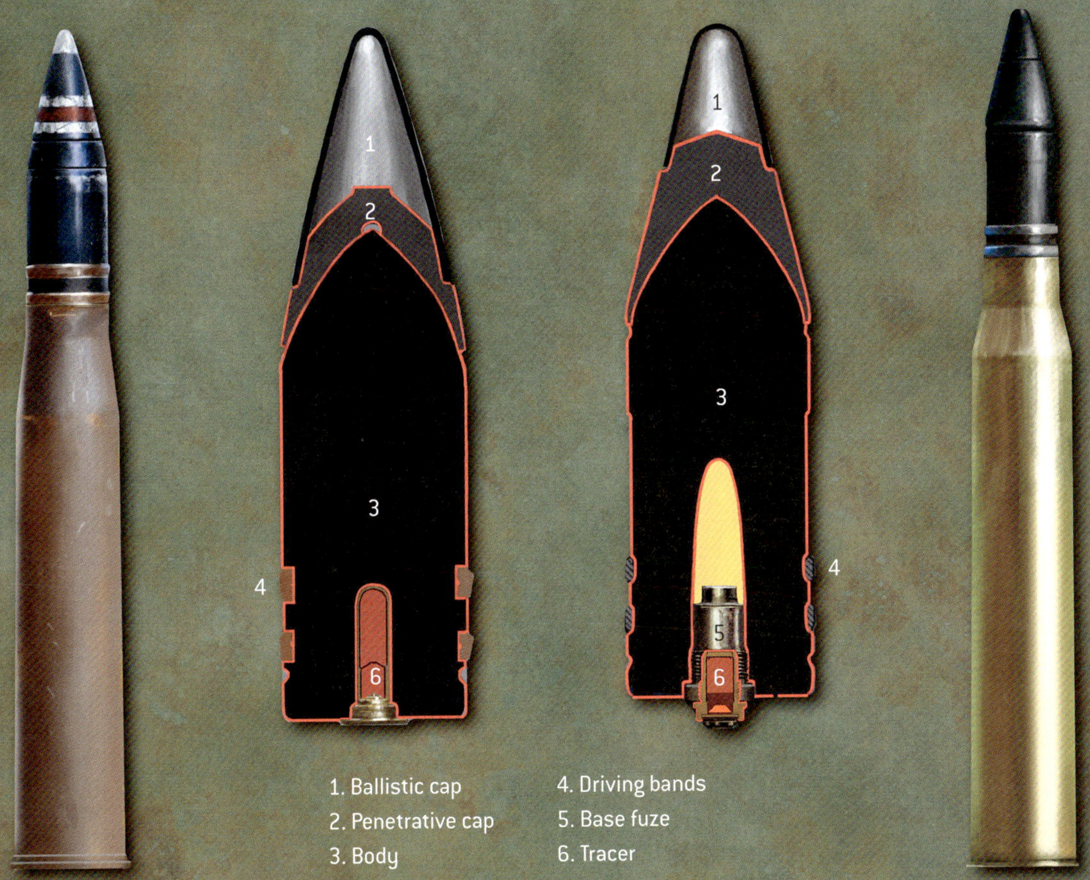

The Challenger fired the APCBC/T (Armour Piercing Capped Ballistic Capped/Tracer) Mk 8 projectile (above left) as its primary anti-tank ammunition. The main body of the projectile was made of steel with a pointed nose to aid penetration into armoured plate.

As there was a danger of the pointed nose shattering on impact, especially against face-hardened armour, a softer blunt-nosed penetrative cap was added to absorb some of the initial impact and give the pointed nose a better chance of digging into the armour without shattering or ricocheting. As the blunt cap caused unwanted drag, a hollow ballistic cap was added to give the projectile a more aerodynamic shape. This cap, also called a windshield, was made of light steel and had no impact on the actual armour penetration of the projectile other than ensuring it retained its velocity over longer distances. A tracer was fitted into the base of the projectile that burned for a few seconds and allowed the fall of the shot to be observed more accurately. The Panther's Panzergranate 39/42 was an APCBC projectile similar to that of the Challenger, the main difference being the inclusion of an explosive charge with delay fuze. This had the intended effect of increasing post-penetration damage by exploding inside the enemy tank and breaking up the projectile into smaller splinters, widening the fragmentation cone compared to a solid shot.

In theory this increased the chance of splinters hitting crew or ammunition, but the fuze was a complicated device and the cavity for the explosive filler risked weakening the projectile, so to withstand the high velocity of the Panther's gun, the explosive filler of the Pzgr 39/42 had to be kept small, which reduced the effectiveness of its burst. The British did not consider the potential damage to be worth the reduced reliability and used a projectile without explosive filler.

A penetration of the Panther's armour had a good chance of causing a catastrophic propellant fire as the large cartridges were spread throughout the crew compartment without protection. Propellant fires were less likely to happen in the Challenger as the British had introduced armoured ammunition stowage bins. These took up space and made the rounds less accessible, but they were successful in keeping out small splinters and increasing crew survivability in the event of a penetrating hit.

FIREPOWER VS UNARMOURED TARGETS

Besides the important but fairly rare task of destroying other tanks, another aspect of tank firepower was neutralizing more common unarmoured targets such as infantry and crew-served weapons. This was an initial shortcoming of British tanks before the introduction of dual-purpose guns, but on the Challenger this mistake was repeated due to its intended role as a dedicated 'hole puncher'.

The 17-pdr was primarily designed as an anti-tank gun and initially lacked a good HE shell. This ammunition was fired at the same velocity as AP ammunition, which gave it a flat trajectory that made hitting low-lying targets difficult. Its thick shell also reduced the internal space for explosive filler and resulted in a poor fragmentation pattern. Complaints from the Normandy front led to the development of a lower-velocity, high-capacity shell with an improved fuze that gave satisfactory performance, but production delays prevented its widespread use before the end of the war. As a stopgap solution, the existing low-capacity shell with its simple fuze could be fired with a reduced-propellant charge to at least give it a better trajectory. Unfortunately for the Challenger its Mk II 17-pdr could not eject the reduced-charge case, so it was decided that Challengers would use up the stockpile of high-velocity HE ammunition while the Fireflies received the more effective low-velocity rounds.

Challenger T271940 was the last to roll off the production line with the original 63mm turret nose plate before this was increased to 102mm, making it the thickest piece of armour on the Challenger. It still could not resist powerful guns such as that mounted in the Panther, but it provided some protection against weaker anti-tank weapons. (piemags/archive/military/Alamy Stock Photo)

A single machine gun was mounted coaxially in the Challenger's turret. The compact American 7.62mm Browning M1919A4 was chosen instead of the bulky 7.92mm Besa usually found on British tanks. For emergency use against aircraft or close-range infantry, a .303 Bren light machine gun was stowed inside the turret.

The Panther was intended to become Germany's next-generation battle tank and required multi-purpose armament capable of effectively dealing with a wide array of targets. Its HE shell, the Sprenggranate 42, had all the features that the 17-pdr shell initially lacked: a lower velocity, greater explosive content, enhanced fragmentation effect and a contact fuze with optional delay setting for ricochet fire or penetration of light cover. The Panther also had a hull machine gun in addition to its coaxial and cupola-mounted machine guns for a total of three 7.92mm MG 34s. A roof-mounted launcher for smoke bombs was similar to the one on the Challenger but could also be used to fire small fragmentation grenades against close-range infantry.

CREW STATIONS

A tank is more than a machine, it is also a fighting position for its crewmembers. A tank's effectiveness is dictated by the ergonomics of the crew stations, the ease of interaction with the tank's controls and the speed of communication. The Panther had a conventional layout of three men in the turret and two in the front of the hull. The Challenger also had five crewmen but seated four in the turret and just one in the hull.

The commander's seat on the Challenger was inconveniently placed in the front right of the turret and was one of the least ergonomic positions. The coaxial machine gun was installed as an afterthought and protruded into the commander's position, distracting him with the loading and maintenance of the weapon. Visibility was limited to just two periscopes on a rotating cupola that was nearly flush with the turret roof and only offered a limited view. In most situations the commander was forced to open up the turret hatch and observe his surroundings with his head exposed. A sighting vane was installed on the turret roof that allowed the commander verbally to guide the gunner in traversing the turret on target, calling out 'steady' when the vane approached the target and 'on' when it was lined up.

Trooper Lyon of Liverpool observes the Challenger's surroundings from his hatch on the left side of the turret roof. Besides his main duty as wireless operator, he is also responsible for loading the main gun in turns with another loader who stands in the right half of the turret. (piemags/archive/military/Alamy Stock Photo)

The commander of the Panther sat in the rear left of the turret on a raised seat. This gave him a good overview of the interior and visual contact with the turret crew. A tall cupola with seven periscopes provided the commander with near-all-round vision of his surroundings without having to expose his head and shoulders. A simple sighting vane could be seen through the front periscope and served the same purpose as on the Challenger. The commander could adopt the exposed method of observing by standing on a footrest with his head outside the turret.

The Panther's gunner was seated directly in front of the commander, allowing for a tap on the shoulder if other means of communication failed. The gunner's station was cramped and lacked an escape hatch. His gunsight was an excellent device that featured a low magnification setting with a wide field of view for target acquisition and a high magnification setting for precise aiming at long range. The sight had a sophisticated articulated construction that kept the eyepiece level while the end of the scope pivoted up or down with the gun. Allied evaluations praised the Panther's gunsight but criticized the lack of a secondary optic for increased situational awareness. To get his bearings the gunner had to look at a small clock near his left hand that indicated the turret position relative to the hull.

The Challenger's gunner was also seated in the front left of the turret without a hatch of his own. His gunsight was not articulated like the Panther's and its single setting combined a low magnification with a narrow field of view. A rotating and tilting periscope offered a wider field of view for target acquisition but a traverse indicator like the Panther's was not installed.

The Challenger's gunner controlled the electrical power-traverse system by turning a spade grip with his left hand. The maximum traverse rate was a very impressive 30 degrees per second but required coordination with the driver to increase engine speed. Fine laying was possible with the power traverse as it had a slow minimum speed and instant stop. The balanced mounting of the 17-pdr gun allowed for easy elevation control via a wheel operated by the gunner's right hand. By contrast the Panther's gun was mounted far forward in the turret and required a complex pneumatic equilibrator to assist with elevation. The Panther's hydraulic power traverse was controlled through a set of foot pedals and also required the driver's assistance to reach its maximum traverse rate of 20 degrees per second. In theory the foot pedals allowed for hands-free aiming, but in practice the control was stiff and unreliable on inclines. Fine laying was best done with the handwheel, which was more precise but slow to turn.

Corporal Potter, hailing from Nottinghamshire, commands his Challenger from an open cupola hatch, a dangerous necessity as the vision from within is limited to just two periscopes. The triangular device protruding from the turret roof is the sighting vane that is aligned with the gunsight so the commander can guide the gunner on target over the intercom. (piemags/archive/military/Alamy Stock Photo)

A30 CHALLENGER TURRET

1. Commander's cupola
2. Loader's periscope
3. Bren gun magazine (100 rounds)
4. Drinking water tank
5. Armoured ammunition bin
6. Loader's seat
7. Traverse indicator
8. Auxiliary foot pedal trigger
9. Gunner's seat
10. Elevation handwheel
11. Hand traverse wheel
12. Power traverse controller
13. Gunsight
14. Bombthrower
15. Gunner's periscope

Trooper Coombs of Cardiff looks out from the driver's seat of his Challenger. It was a lonely station compared to the Cromwell as the co-driver was omitted to make room for more ammunition. The circular visor was closed in combat, restricting vision to two periscopes that could rotate and tilt in different directions. (piemags/archive/military/Alamy Stock Photo)

On both tanks the gun was fired electrically by a trigger on the handle of the elevating wheel. The Panther had a dedicated foot pedal for firing the coaxial machine gun while the Challenger used a foot pedal as a mechanical back-up trigger for the main gun that could also be set to fire the coaxial machine gun.

The biggest difference between the two tanks' crew stations was the controversial decision to add a second loader to the Challenger. The loaders stood on either side of the gun breech in the rear of the turret and each had easy access to an ammunition stowage bin containing three rounds. Getting hold of the remaining 42 rounds required help from other crewmembers. The Challenger was not designed with the longer APCBC ammunition in mind so not all ammunition stowage bins could accommodate them and the rounds were impossible to load if the gun was depressed too far. The right-hand loader stood next to the commander and was responsible for the operation of the gun. He released the safety switch, communicated the status of the gun and remedied misfires. The left-hand loader doubled as the wireless operator for the No. 19 Wireless Set that was installed in the rear of the turret. It provided the intercom within the tank, had a short-range set for troop communication and a long-range set for squadron or regimental messages.

The single loader in the Panther was not even connected to the intercom. He did have an impressive 82 rounds of ammunition to work with but none of these rotated along with the turret basket, meaning his access to the rounds depended on the bearing of the turret. This could be quite good at some angles but terrible at others.

Despite the different layouts the reload rate for both tanks averaged around six seconds. This was due to the Panther providing its single loader with sufficient working room and easy access to the gun while the Challenger was unnecessarily cramped by the second loader and inconvenient guardrails.

The radio in the Panther had a dedicated operator who sat in the front right of the hull next to the driver. As a secondary task he fired the hull machine gun. The main radio set was the Fu 5 that also facilitated the intercom. Tanks of the platoon and company commanders had an additional Fu 2 receiver so they could monitor the frequency of a higher command in addition to their own.

In both tanks the driver sat in the front of the hull. His position was low to the ground compared to the turret crew stations and only offered limited visibility to the front. In the Panther Ausf G the driver's optics were reduced to a single rotating

PANTHER AUSF G TURRET

1. Loader's periscope
2. Close-defence weapon
3. Loader's auxiliary hand traverse
4. Turret lock
5. Commander's folding footrest
6. Air compressor
7. Emergency main gun trigger
8. Coaxial machine gun trigger
9. Power traverse foot pedals
10. Power traverse gear ratio lever
11. Hand traverse wheel
12. Elevation handwheel
13. Gunner's traverse indicator
14. Gunsight
15. Coaxial machine gun belt guide

The Panther's circular cupola hatch was mounted on a vertical shaft that could be lowered into a fully closed position or raised into a semi-open position using a rotating handle. Once raised to the semi-open position as shown here, a lever could swing and lock the hatch to the side to fully open it. (Tank Museum TM 0915-A1)

and tilting periscope while the Challenger had two periscopes in addition to a circular port in the visor plate that could be opened up when not in combat. The controls for both tanks were similar. Gear shifting was manual although the Panther had a synchromesh gearbox that alleviated the need for double-declutching. Both tanks used a form of differential steering that was controlled through levers. The turning radius depended on the selected gear and became progressively wider as higher gears were engaged, requiring the driver to shift down for a tight turn. In neutral the tracks could be powered in opposite directions, causing the tank to turn in place. Both tanks only had a single reverse gear with a poor maximum speed that hindered a quick retreat.

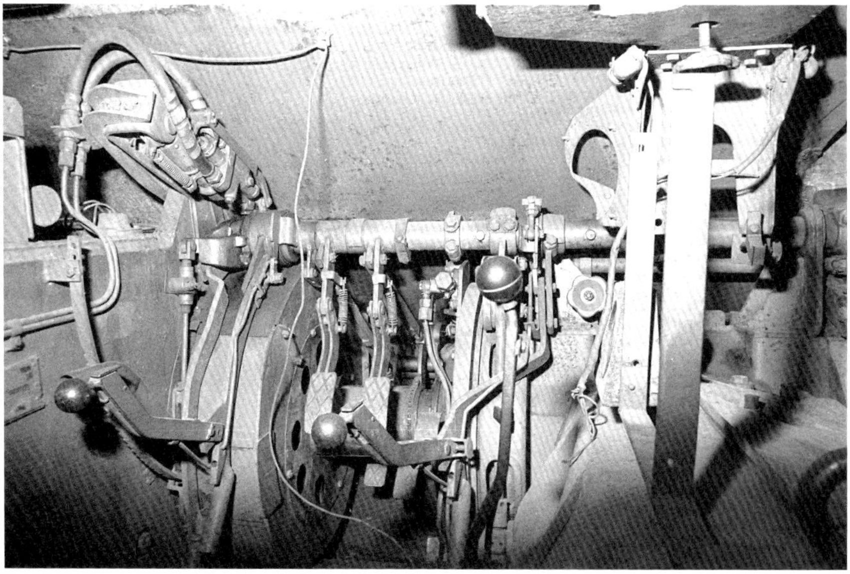

The driver's vision port in the glacis was removed on the Panther Ausf G, leaving him a single periscope. This proved inadequate, so in October 1944 a second, elevated seat and extended controls were introduced so the driver could operate the Panther with his head and shoulders outside his hatch for better visibility when not in combat. (Tank Museum TM 0915-E1)

THE COMBATANTS

TACTICS

By 1944, tank tactics were combined-arms tactics. The optimistic predictions of interwar theorists that tanks could win battles on their own had given way to the sober realization that tanks required close cooperation with the other arms to survive on the battlefield. Infantry had to sweep trenches, woods and buildings of opposing infantry with man-portable anti-tank weapons; flexible artillery fire had to neutralize anti-tank guns quickly and accurately; and engineers had to help the tanks over obstacles and through minefields. In return, the tank provided the combined-arms team with a unique combination of mobile protected firepower that enabled the attack to succeed in the face of modern defensive firepower. There were occasions, however, when the actions of tanks drew in enemy tanks and a tank-on-tank battle ensued. This was comparatively rare and usually included the involvement of other arms, but when tanks encountered enemy tanks, it was nevertheless vital that they were dealt with quickly and decisively. To achieve this, British and German tankers based their tactics on similar fundamental principles that had evolved through years of combat.

It was well understood that a stationary and concealed tank had a major advantage over a tank that was moving out in the open. Improved situational awareness and a stable firing platform allowed the ambusher to spot first, fire first, most likely hit first and keep up a rapid rate of fire. It also gave weaker tanks greater control over the engagement by letting heavier tanks get close or expose their flanks before opening fire. One British manual compared a battle between tanks to the children's game of Hide and Seek as both sides tried to locate the other without

being spotted in the process. The terrain played a key part in this as woods or buildings offered concealment and hills provided cover. Slopes in particular were key features as they allowed tanks to move from a fully covered 'turret down' observation position into a partially covered 'hull down' firing position at the crest, then reverse back again to reposition safely for the next shot. Recognizing such opportunities in the landscape at first glance distinguished the experienced tank commanders from the rookies and it was not uncommon for a battle-hardened leader to dismount and reconnoitre a position on foot before guiding his tank in.

These principles naturally favoured the defender. Attacking with tanks in the face of enemy tanks required disciplined bounds between units to ensure that every high-risk move was covered by a static element, thereby providing some of the benefits of the defence to an offensive action. As one element advanced to a predetermined position, another element stayed in an overwatch position and covered the move. Should the moving tanks receive fire, the static tanks were already in a position to retaliate. Upon completion of the move, the advancing element went 'firm' on their new position and became the overwatch element for the next move that was then carried out by the element that had previously conducted the overwatch. This 'leapfrogging' could be conducted by a pair of tanks or by entire squadrons depending on the situation.

A mixture of Cromwells and Sherman Fireflies identifies this as a column of 22 Armoured Brigade, part of 7th Armoured Division. The Firefly was an unpopular addition to a troop of Cromwells as it stood out and was slower, but it was better than having no 17-pdr at all. (Central Press/Hulton Archive/Getty Images)

Both offensive and defensive tactics were made simpler by a uniformity of tanks. A platoon of Panthers consisted of nothing but Panthers and their identical characteristics gave them tactical flexibility, because the first Panther to spot a target was just as capable of engaging it as any other. For a troop of three Cromwells with a single Challenger in tow, however, the asymmetry in their firepower demanded more complex tactics when heavy enemy armour was encountered.

The British preferred small troops of three tanks for the flexible triangle formations that this enabled, but the inclusion of a fourth tank as 'hole puncher' complicated matters. One solution was to split the troop into two pairs of tanks, the leader usually

The first encounter with a Panther outside Argentan on 19 August came as a shock to 15/19 Hussars, but by the next day the Germans had been driven from the town by US forces. The wreck of a Panther was left among the ruins, its glacis pockmarked by deflected shots. (NARA)

advancing in bounds with the junior tank commander while the troop sergeant formed the second pair with the 17-pdr tank. Regardless of formation, it was best practice to keep the 'hole puncher' in the rear until it was absolutely needed while the regular tanks spearheaded the advance and dealt with unarmoured or lightly armoured targets. If they spotted an enemy tank that they could not frontally penetrate or easily outflank, they called up their 'hole puncher' with detailed instructions on the target and suitable firing positions.

This battle drill was demonstrated by Lieutenant C.C. Egerton's 3 Tp, A Sqn, 15/19 Hussars, when it encountered German resistance south-east of the Dutch village of Liessel on 24 September 1944. The lead Cromwell under command of Corporal Nicholls was advancing down a road when it was struck by a high-velocity gun and caught fire. Egerton moved up to reconnoitre and thought he spotted a camouflaged tank in a treeline so he called for his Challenger under command of Sergeant Gadd. The Challenger took up a concealed position behind a high hedge that obstructed its view, so Egerton had to help guide it on target from an exposed position. The Challenger had only fired once or twice before a German gun zeroed in on its prominent muzzle flash and struck the Challenger in the turret, killing two crewmen. It was later discovered that Egerton had misidentified the enemy tank and that they were actually fighting 88mm FlaK guns. Egerton's troop fought with skill and bravery, but they could not overcome the weaknesses of the Challenger. It was a single, high-priority target that took time and coordination to move into position. Its high profile made it difficult to hide and the powerful 17-pdr gunfire quickly drew enemy return fire that the Challenger's thin armour could not resist.

15/19 HUSSARS

The result of a merger of two cavalry regiments in 1922, 15/19 Hussars had exchanged horses for armour in 1938 and took part in the ill-fated Battle of France (May–June 1940). After making it back across the Channel, 15/19 Hussars was rebuilt as a cruiser tank-equipped armoured regiment and remained in Britain until the summer of 1944. In April 1943 the regiment was one of the first units to receive the new A27M Cromwell and related A27L Centaur cruiser tanks for testing. During this time the manpower of 15/19 Hussars was constantly changing as new men came in for training before being sent on to units fighting overseas, but the most promising recruits were retained by the regiment.

With D-Day looming, in May 1944 the unit was fully equipped with the latest Cromwells and eager to go into action, but shortly before the invasion of Normandy was launched the regiment was selected for secret training in amphibious Sherman tanks. The conversion was only just completed in August when the mission was changed again and the regiment was ordered to Normandy to become the armoured reconnaissance regiment of 11th Armoured Division, a role that would make 15/19 Hussars one of the few units to receive the Challenger.

A tank commander of 15/19 Hussars has his picture taken by a Dutch civilian in Eindhoven on 19 September. Headphones muffled sounds and produced a static buzz, so they were usually not worn directly over the ears when talking to people outside the tank. (RHC Eindhoven 20209/0139878)

Years of combat experience had resulted in the evolution of the British armoured division into a balanced combined-arms formation. Its two principal components were an armoured brigade consisting of three battalion-sized armoured regiments backed up by an armoured-infantry battalion and an infantry brigade of three motorized-infantry battalions. These two brigades received fire support from Royal Artillery (RA) units including an anti-tank regiment fielding 17-pdr guns in both towed and self-propelled configurations. The divisional armoured reconnaissance regiment stood outside the structure of the armoured brigade as it was intended to provide close reconnaissance for the armoured division as a whole and was sufficiently strong to fight for information, which in practice made the armoured reconnaissance regiment little different from the division's regular armoured regiments.

In terms of equipment the British and Polish armoured reconnaissance regiments in North-West Europe were outfitted with Cromwells while most regular armoured regiments made use of the more numerous American Sherman. The only exception was 7th Armoured Division, which fielded the Cromwell in all four of its armoured regiments. The resulting total of six Cromwell-equipped regiments across the three armoured divisions of the British Second Army led to a demand for 72 Challengers, but fewer than 30 had been produced in time for D-Day. It was therefore decided that the three armoured reconnaissance regiments would get the Challengers while the three regular armoured regiments of

Life outside the Challenger mainly took place just behind the front in leaguers, also known as harbours, where the crews performed maintenance, replenished fuel and ammunition and received briefings on the next day's actions. By the time all this was done, only a few hours for rest remained. (Tank Museum TM 2464-D6)

7th Armoured Division would have to use Fireflies alongside their Cromwells as they had previous experience in the Sherman. The 1st Czechoslovak Independent Armoured Brigade and the armoured reconnaissance regiment of the Polish 1st Armoured Division also used Cromwells and received their full allotment of Challengers later in the war.

An armoured reconnaissance regiment consisted of A, B and C squadrons supported by an HQ squadron that included a reconnaissance 'squadron' of 11 scout cars. The HQ squadron had the demanding task of administering the regiment and ensuring the smooth flow of supplies and information in hectic and mobile conditions. The three fighting squadrons shared the same organization of a headquarters and four troops. The major in command of a squadron had a regular Cromwell while the squadron's captain and sergeant major had close-support versions armed with a 95mm howitzer. Rounding out the squadron's headquarters was a recovery Cromwell for towing away immobilized tanks. Each squadron was trailed by its own supply echelon with enough capacity to replenish the fighting vehicles fully after one average day of combat.

The smallest tactical units were the four troops that made up each squadron. A troop consisted of four tanks under the command of a lieutenant. Three of the tanks were regular Cromwells and the fourth was a Challenger for a total of 12 Challengers throughout the regiment. The dispersed troop integration was not popular with some units that had not faced heavy German armour before and preferred to separate their unwieldy 'hole punchers' into dedicated troops or even a squadron, but experience in Normandy quickly showed the importance of having a 17-pdr close at hand down at the troop level.

On 19 August 1944, 15/19 Hussars would learn this lesson the hard way during its first day in action. The regiment had collected its equipment just three days earlier when it arrived in Normandy and was only given two days to prepare for battle before a long journey by road would bring it to its new home in 11th Armoured Division. The regiment's tankers had no prior experience with the Challenger and a mere two days were insufficient for crew familiarization, let alone tactical training with the rest of the troop.

On 19 August the battle-hardened 11th Armoured Division was pushing into the mass of German forces trapped in the Falaise Pocket. It was a fine sunny day and 15/19 Hussars had a fairly calm first time in action providing flank protection to the west of Argentan. As evening approached B Sqn ventured out to engage retreating German columns to its east. Some tanks experienced mechanical trouble, likely caused by the hasty handover from the depot, and the squadron drew the attention of German snipers and mortar spotters as it awaited repairs. The situation escalated dramatically when a single Panther appeared and effortlessly destroyed the Cromwell of Lieutenant J.R.D. Sharpe, the 1 Tp leader, killing Corporal F. Edwards and severely injuring the four other crewmen. A duel ensued in the rolling hills as other troops pushed in on the lone Panther. Lieutenant S.R.M. Frazer led his 4 Tp up to a crest and saw the Panther in the low ground less than 400m to his front. Seven times he ordered his driver into a firing position and seven times his gunner hit the Panther on its turret. Each time the Cromwell's AP shot bounced upward off the mantlet and on the seventh attempt Frazer tried his luck with an HE shell. On the eighth venture into a firing position he had lost sight of the Panther in a nearby copse.

Lieutenant-Colonel Taylor receives the Distinguished Service Order for his daring leadership of 15/19 Hussars during Operation *Market Garden*. The investiture was held by Field Marshal Montgomery on 22 January 1945 in the Dutch town of Weert. Taylor had previously received the Military Cross for his escape from German captivity in 1940. (piemags/ww2archive/Alamy Stock Photo)

By nightfall the demoralized squadron was ordered to withdraw. Radio communication broke down and vehicles became bogged in unfamiliar terrain, with eight of the tanks being abandoned by their nervous crews. The encounter confirmed the inadequacy of the Cromwell in a direct confrontation with the Panther, a mismatch that Lieutenant Frazer likened to 'David and Goliath'. Notably absent from the accounts of the battle are the Challengers of B Sqn. Inexperience likely played a key part in their underutilization as the quick intervention of a 'hole puncher' at the right place and time required ingrained battle drills that would naturally be lacking during a first combat encounter with unfamiliar equipment.

Luckily for 15/19 Hussars its first action was also one of the last that the Germans trapped in the Falaise Pocket could manage and in the following weeks Allied forces surged through France and Belgium. The fast and reliable Cromwells and Challengers were in their element and the 15/19 Hussars gained valuable experience. By early

September the Netherlands–Belgium border was reached and German resistance sharply increased. Mounting losses to concealed guns, man-portable launchers and mines were a painful reminder to the tankers that the war was far from over. The battle-hardened regiment left 11th Armoured Division on 12 September to join XXX Corps in the tiny bridgehead across the Maas–Schelde Canal that would serve as the springboard for Operation *Market Garden*. On 14 September, Sergeant M. Hollis of C Sqn played a key role in repulsing a German attack on the salient by destroying three StuG III assault guns in quick succession. Three days later 15/19 Hussars was on the attack again as part of *Market Garden*.

ANTHONY DONNITHORNE TAYLOR

Anthony D. Taylor (1910–85) joined 15/19 Hussars in 1930 at the age of 20. In May 1940 he served as the regiment's adjutant when he was captured by German forces during the invasion of France and the Low Countries. Over the course of 20 days, Taylor escaped from captivity twice and eventually reached the Channel where he was rescued by the Royal Navy and safely returned to England and the remnants of his regiment. Taylor was given command of 15/19 Hussars in August 1942 and led the regiment throughout the North-West Europe campaign.

During the fighting around Son, Lieutenant-Colonel Taylor again found himself behind enemy lines. At 0500hrs on 20 September 1944, he was summoned to the command post of the US 101st Airborne Division in the Son Catholic community centre. The building and neighbouring church tower had caught the attention of Panther gunners the previous evening and suffered multiple direct hits with HE shells. Taylor was briefed about the situation and the need for a quick counter-attack to drive back the German tanks. Looking at a map, the same minor crossing over the Dommel River near the Hooidonk watermill that interested the Germans, also caught Taylor's attention. With his usual penchant for daring reconnaissance actions, Taylor ordered his B Sqn and C Sqn to prepare for battle while he set off in his armoured scout car with Lieutenant T.C.A. Goldsmith in the driver's seat. They headed south across the Bailey bridge, drove past the wreckage of last evening's Panzer raid, and swung onto a narrow by-road that ran between the main road and the Dommel. There they encountered two jeeps of the 101st Airborne Division's reconnaissance platoon led by Captain T.P. Wilder. After a brief conversation it was decided to investigate the bridge together. With the scout car in the lead the small column continued down the curving trail in the early morning mist.

As they approached the track junction that would take them left to the watermill, Lieutenant Goldsmith stopped the scout car. In the dim light they could see something snaking through the distant mist. The British and American officers dismounted for a better look. A column of troops was marching through a ditch, but their helmets gave them the appearance of Americans. Another mystery column appeared out of the mist and silently marched across the junction just five paces away. One soldier nodded a greeting to Taylor, who suddenly realized that he was looking at German *Fallschirmjäger*. Taylor briefly entertained the thought of capturing the Germans, but by now he had seen over 200 heavily armed men march past and he quickly abandoned the idea in favour of a quick escape. The officers cautiously returned to their vehicles and reversed down the narrow road. This alarmed the Germans and a salvo of small-arms fire rang out. The armoured scout car deflected the rounds and shielded the jeeps behind it as they reversed past a bend in the trail. Taylor raced back to Son where he exchanged his scout car for a Cromwell to lead his regiment into battle.

Lieutenant-Colonel Taylor's German counterpart in Panzer-Brigade 107, Major Hans-Albrecht von Plüskow of Panzer-Abteilung 2107, also led from the front. When the brigade carried out its second assault on the Allied corridor further north at Veghel on 23 September 1944, a Sherman tank of 44 RTR caught his command Panther in the flank. A rapid sequence of three hits knocked off a track, hit Plüskow in the head and penetrated the turret, setting his tank on fire. Leading from the front could inspire a unit or leave it leaderless at a crucial moment.

PANZER-BRIGADE 107

Confronting 15/19 Hussars for control of the Operation *Market Garden* corridor was Panzer-Brigade 107. This unit, along with nine others of its kind, was raised in July 1944 in an attempt to reform Germany's dwindling tank fleet following heavy losses on the Eastern Front. Instead of merging scarce Panthers and armoured half-tracks into large *Panzer-Divisionen*, it was hoped that concentrating these valuable assets into smaller *Panzer-Brigaden* would allow them to punch above their weight through speed and surprise. While tactically offensive, their strategic role was to bolster Germany's crumbling defences by creating a large number of small but mobile brigades to counter-attack enemy breakthroughs and stabilize the front line.

This narrow scope was reflected in the brigade's streamlined organization of just two major parts: a *Panzer-Abteilung* (tank battalion) and a *Panzergrenadier-Bataillon* (armoured-infantry battalion). The downsized tank battalion had 36 Panther tanks in three companies of 11 tanks each, organized in three platoons of three tanks and a company headquarters with two tanks. Three command Panthers with special radios were allotted to battalion headquarters. A fourth company had to make do with 11 Jagdpanzer IV/70 tank destroyers. These boasted armour and firepower similar to the Panther but lacked the flexibility of a rotating turret and had to rely on their lower profile to serve a more passive ambush role. A support company provided the battalion with supplies, maintenance and medical care. The brigade's other half was the armoured-infantry battalion. Some of the squads were fully equipped with new assault rifles and the half-tracks carried an assortment of heavy weaponry ranging from triple autocannons to howitzers and mortars. Additional brigade assets included a company of *Pioniere* (assault engineers) with flamethrowing half-tracks and sections of self-propelled anti-aircraft guns.

While packing a lot of punch for a fairly small unit, the deliberate downsizing came at the cost of flexibility and sustainability. Gone was the combined-arms approach that had

A *Panzerbefehlswagen* variant of the Panther navigates the narrow Norman *bocage*. This command tank was easily distinguished from the regular Panther by the prominent star antenna protruding from the rear of the engine deck. Internal modifications included the removal of the coaxial MG 34 machine gun to make room for additional radio equipment. (michael cremin/Alamy Stock Photo)

made the German *Panzer-Division* such a force to be reckoned with. The *Panzer-Brigade* lacked artillery and only possessed rudimentary reconnaissance and engineering assets. Its direct firepower was impressive, but included weapons of varying calibres that burdened the supply chain. The brigade's supply echelon of 20 trucks with a total capacity of 60 tonnes was inadequate for any kind of sustained action and repair facilities were similarly too limited for a unit with over 150 combat vehicles. In theory the brigades may have performed well within their intended role of quick counter-attacks over familiar terrain and with the support of nearby units, but in practice many brigades were haphazardly thrown into battle, worn down to a stump and disbanded within months of their creation.

BERNDT-JOACHIM FREIHERR VON MALTZAHN

Berndt-Joachim von Maltzahn (1903–64) was born into a centuries-old noble lineage and served as a cavalry officer at the start of World War II. He proved himself a brave and capable commander who was adored by his men and praised by his superiors. The command of Panzer-Brigade 107 was entrusted to Maltzahn based on his previous experience, but his overly cautious handling of the unit quickly led to the search for a more aggressive replacement. Maltzahn relinquished command of the brigade on 14 October 1944.

Maltzahn's troubles as commander of Panzer-Brigade 107 began soon after he boarded the first of 17 trains that carried his brigade west on 16 September 1944. The journey from Mielau in Poland to Aachen in Germany took an unexpected turn the next day when the German high command rerouted the brigade to the Netherlands following the sudden Allied offensive. In the early morning hours of 18 September, Maltzahn found himself in the train station of Venlo, a Dutch town close to the border with Germany. The station was abandoned save for a few sleepy railway officials. Maltzahn knew nothing of the situation and had to send out men to contact nearby units for information.

Eventually the headquarters of the 1. Fallschirmarmee under Generaloberst Kurt Student could be reached by telephone and Maltzahn received orders to report to the LXXXVI. Armeekorps under General der Infanterie Hans von Obstfelder. As soon as a staff car was unloaded Maltzahn travelled to Hillenraad Castle near Roermond where he was briefed on the situation and given orders to march to Eindhoven and block the British armoured advance that was still south of the city. Maltzahn pleaded for more time to unload his brigade, pointing out that its clearly defined role necessitated a concentrated strike, not a piecemeal deployment. The corps commander relented and also promised to provide fuel. To speed up unloading some trains passed Venlo and went to Roermond, splitting the brigade until it could regroup at the village of Meijel on its way to the front.

Maltzahn returned to Venlo around midday. Assembly was progressing slowly due to the threat of air attack and the need to keep forces dispersed in the shadows. The second train containing Panthers and half-tracks was still being unloaded when Maltzahn received a message from the LXXXVI. Armeekorps ordering him to attack immediately. Maltzahn rang corps command to explain the folly of such demands when not a single one of his companies had fully assembled and the order was once again postponed. By evening the first companies had finally formed up when Obstfelder himself called demanding an attack on the Son bridge early the next day with whatever elements were available by then.

Unloading progressed more quickly under the cover of darkness and the bulk of the combat elements had assembled before daybreak on 19 September, but the supply echelon was trailing behind and would not finish unloading until the evening. The fuel promised by the LXXXVI. Armeekorps had not arrived either, so Maltzahn resorted to draining his administrative lorries of their petrol to top up his armoured vehicles for the long drive to Son. The brigade set out as ordered and by the late afternoon of the 19th Maltzahn had reached the small village of Nederwetten where he established his command post in the pub at the fork in the road. Maps were examined on the billiard table and soon dispatch riders were streaming out of Nederwetten carrying orders for the attack.

Wireless communication was an essential prerequisite for armoured warfare, but poor reliability and risk of interception meant that meeting in person remained the best method of issuing detailed orders. German tank units usually relied on half-tracks with decent off-road mobility for intercommunication, while the British preferred fast scout cars as 'runabouts'. (michael cremin/Alamy Stock Photo)

Panzer-Brigade 107 was established, outfitted and trained in just six weeks. In late July 1944 a nucleus of survivors from the shattered 25. Panzergrenadier-Division was brought to the massive training facility near Mielau in occupied Poland and reinforced with personnel from replacement units. Officers and specialist mechanics went back to Germany for courses while the bulk of the tank crews received basic military training until the first Panthers trickled in starting on 23 August. Gunnery and tactical training began in earnest in September but only lasted a few days and remained limited in scope to company exercises. One full-scale brigade exercise was held on 8 September although the *Jagdpanzer* company and many transport vehicles were still missing and would only arrive mere days before the brigade departed for the front. Manpower was comparatively abundant and the overstaffed brigade even established a small replacement company. Despite the hasty establishment the brigade commander, Major Berndt-Joachim Freiherr von Maltzahn, valued his unit highly, boasting of picked men in key positions and better preparedness than the short training period would suggest.

On 16 September, Panzer-Brigade 107 set out for the Western Front by rail, unaware that it was the eve of a daring Allied offensive into which the brigade would soon be drawn.

In addition to its three companies of Panther tanks, Panzer-Brigade 107 also fielded a company of 11 Jagdpanzer IV/70 tank destroyers. Despite utilizing the ageing PzKpfw IV chassis, the Jagdpanzer mounted the same powerful gun as the Panther behind a comparable level of frontal protection, but had to sacrifice the flexibility offered by a turret to do so. (Imperial War Museums via Getty Images)

THE STRATEGIC SITUATION

Operation *Market Garden* was launched on 17 September 1944 at a time when Allied confidence in a swift victory was at an all-time high. After nearly two months of attritional combat in the Normandy beachhead they had finally broken out, encircled a large German force in the Falaise Pocket and were racing through France and Belgium towards the German heartland. From the border with Switzerland to the Channel, a seemingly unstoppable mass of Allied men and *matériel* was sweeping aside shattered German forces.

As *Market Garden* was locked into its final planning phase by 10 September, the situation on the ground was beginning to shift. American forces were running into the concrete defences of the Siegfried Line that shielded the German frontier and British troops encountered renewed resistance behind the waterways along the Netherlands–Belgium border. Allied supply lines were stretched to breaking point while the looming autumn weather brought with it fears of a static front line mired in mud.

To maintain their forward momentum the Allies decided to concentrate on a big push along a narrow front to secure a lodgement across the formidable Rhine River and set the conditions for a future offensive against Germany's vital Ruhr industrial area. Field Marshal B.L. Montgomery successfully advocated for an offensive by British Second Army into the Netherlands with the support of Allied airborne forces waiting on English airfields. These elite troops had proven their worth in Normandy and formed a reserve of divisions that could be dropped onto the mainland without congesting the already overburdened supply lines. Their air landings would fall under codename *Market* and the simultaneous ground advance under *Garden*. In seven days the details of the war's largest airborne offensive were worked out with a sense of optimism that would not survive the operation.

OPERATION *GARDEN*

Spearheading Operation *Garden* was the British XXX Corps consisting of the Guards Armoured Division, two infantry divisions (43rd and 50th) and supporting units. The mission of the Guardsmen was a familiar one: blast through the German defences with overwhelming firepower, then exploit the breach with a rapid advance into the enemy rear. The breakthrough had to be made out of a tiny bridgehead across the Maas–Schelde Canal and the drive would end on the shore of the IJsselmeer lake 150km to the north. If successful the operation would trap significant German forces to the west in the Netherlands and set the conditions for a follow-up operation to the east into the North German Plain. To reach this ambitious goal XXX Corps had to cross multiple large waterways with bridges that could easily be destroyed by local German garrisons. That is why a 'carpet' of airborne forces would be rolled out along the XXX Corps route to capture the bridges intact.

An odd inclusion in the order of battle was 15/19 Hussars and its Challenger tanks. The regiment had been detached from 11th Armoured Division on 12 September to help secure the XXX Corps bridgehead across the Maas–Schelde Canal so the Guards Armoured Division could pull out and prepare for Operation *Garden*. On 17 September the regiment was tasked with assisting the breakout battle by supporting infantry attacks on the shoulders of the breach. The opposition was a motley collection of German forces known as Kampfgruppe Walther. While generously classed as a division by Allied intelligence, the German battlegroup's actual strength resembled a security screen that could not stand up to the concentrated firepower the British were planning to unleash upon it.

One of the three Challengers that 2 Northamptonshire Yeomanry received shortly before the regiment's disbandment passes through Flers in Normandy on 17 August 1944. The unit's role as 11th Armoured Division's armoured reconnaissance regiment was taken over by 15/19 Hussars the following day. The three Challengers were also handed over to bolster the 11 the 15/19 Hussars had received upon arrival in Normandy. (piemags/archive/military/Alamy Stock Photo)

For 15/19 Hussars, the first two days of the operation were spent securing the breach and on 19 September the regiment was to follow the Guards and link up with the southernmost airborne force, the US 101st Airborne Division in the Eindhoven area. The regiment would assist the light airborne infantry in keeping open a narrow corridor for XXX Corps to advance through until the other two corps of British Second Army had rolled up the flanks. Its XII Corps to the west and VIII Corps to the east would attack alongside XXX Corps but at a slower pace as they did not have airborne forces clearing their way. It was expected that VIII Corps would come up level with the eastern flank of the 101st Airborne Division's sector after several days, at which point 15/19 Hussars would revert to its place in the 11th Armoured Division that was spearheading the VIII Corps advance.

Sherman tanks of the Guards Armoured Division, including a Firefly with its long 17-pdr gun, advance over the recently captured Waal bridge in Nijmegen. Despite its limited overall width, up-gunning the Sherman was relatively easy as it had a wide turret ring and fairly spacious interior thanks to the panniers that extended the upper part of the hull over the tracks. (NARA)

OPERATION *MARKET*

The airborne operation codenamed *Market* was a highly ambitious plan based on the optimistic assumption that the Wehrmacht was all but beaten and could not organize an effective defence against sudden massed airborne landings in its rear-areas. The British 1st Airborne Division and Polish 1st Parachute Brigade would land far to the north around Arnhem to secure the Rhine crossings. The US 82d Airborne Division would land further south near Nijmegen and capture the bridges over the Waal and Maas. Finally, the US 101st Airborne Division would secure a number of crossings over minor rivers and canals in the far south between Eindhoven and Veghel. Not even 1,500 transport aircraft could deliver the mass of men and *matériel* in a single lift, however, so multiple drops were planned over the course of several days. Betting on consistent flying weather in the middle of September was risky and even if the drops went according to schedule, the initial strike would be diluted by the need to guard the drop zones for reinforcements.

The first wave of Major General Maxwell D. Taylor's 101st Airborne Division landed in their southern sector on 17 September under perfect conditions. The risky daylight drop had paid off as losses were minimal and three full parachute infantry regiments (PIRs) quickly fanned out to their objectives. In the south the 506th PIR seized the village of Son after a brief battle but could not prevent the destruction of the bridge over the Wilhelmina Canal. By the next day the 506th PIR had forded the canal and liberated the city of Eindhoven from the north. On the evening of 18 September the Guards Armoured Division had also fought its way into the city from the south and the first link-up between armour and airborne was a fact. British engineers spent the night building a Bailey bridge over the Wilhelmina Canal at Son and by the morning of the 19th the spearhead of XXX Corps was racing north to Nijmegen.

The Panther boasted a balanced combination of mobility, protection and firepower that made it well-suited for a variety of missions. British reports classed the Panther as a 'heavy cruiser', a designation that was also applied to the British A41 Centurion when it was first proposed in 1943. (Imwar/Alamy Stock Photo)

The 101st Airborne Division now switched to a defensive footing to protect the narrow corridor from German counter-attacks. At the southern boundary of the division's sector the single road to Arnhem snaked through the narrow city streets of Eindhoven and over the winding Dommel River. It then ran directly north from the city and crossed the Wilhelmina Canal at Son, swung through Sint-Oedenrode and again crossed the Dommel, continued to Veghel where it spanned the Zuid-Willemsvaart Canal and Aa River and went on to the town of Uden that marked the division's northern boundary.

Much-needed reinforcements arrived on 19 September in the form of 15/19 Hussars with under its command the armoured cars of A Sqn, 1 Royal Dragoons, and self-propelled artillery of 341 Bty, 86 Fd Regt RA. Later that day 44 Royal Tank Regiment (RTR) with its Sherman tanks would arrive, giving the 101st Airborne Division two battalions' worth of tanks.

These reinforcements had arrived in the nick of time because the German response to *Market Garden* was swifter and more vigorous than anticipated – and it was the bridge at Son that attracted their particular attention. By 19 September the advance of XXX Corps was hanging by a thread as the two flank corps were lagging behind. The result was a vulnerable bottleneck at Son where the recently constructed Bailey bridge carried the full weight of XXX Corps. If the Germans could sever the narrow lifeline at Son where it was most vulnerable, they would encircle all Allied forces to the north of the cut and hold Operation *Market Garden* in a fatal stranglehold. Vicious fighting was already taking place in the woods west of the village when Panther tanks suddenly appeared from the east.

COMBAT

OPENING MOVES, 19 SEPTEMBER 1944

At 1000hrs on 19 September, 15/19 Hussars entered Eindhoven and slowly made its way through jubilant crowds welcoming their liberators. The regiment's A Sqn and the attached squadron of 1 Royal Dragoons remained in the city under command of the 506th PIR while the rest moved up the road to Son and reported to Major General Taylor in his divisional command post. Taylor's biggest concern at the time was to the west, where the stubbornly defended village of Best formed a staging area

'Eindhoven was an unforgettable sight. The streets were thronged with people, densely packed to watch us all go by,' wrote Major G. Courage of the hero's welcome 15/19 Hussars received on 19 September. That evening the Luftwaffe bombed Eindhoven, killing 227 civilians and two members of the regiment. (RHC Eindhoven 20096/0064685)

A Cromwell and Challenger of 15/19 Hussars snake through the streets of Eindhoven on their way to Son, sometime before midday on 19 September. The Challenger carries the markings of C Sqn's 4 Tp. The following day it would fire a knock-out shot into the flank of a Panther. (RHC Eindhoven 20223/0064657)

for German counter-attacks against his landing zones. Gliders with much-needed reinforcements including heavy weapons were scheduled to come in that afternoon, so Taylor wanted the Germans driven back. The tanks of B Sqn and C Sqn fought a battle in the woods around Best that lasted until sundown and came at the cost of two Cromwells, a Challenger and ten crew casualties. The Cromwells had been hit by concealed guns and the Challenger was ambushed by an infantry anti-tank team. This happened shortly before dark and the Germans managed to capture the Challenger to examine it.

Meanwhile in Eindhoven, A Sqn had a lot of ground to cover and split-up in 'Pearson Force' under the squadron commander, Major M. Pearson, and 'Weatherby Force' named after the 24-year-old second-in-command, Captain C.N. Weatherby. Both task forces were accompanied by squads of American paratroopers riding on the tanks. Together with the armoured cars of 1 Royal Dragoons the two task forces spent a fairly quiet afternoon patrolling the city outskirts. Weatherby Force saw the most action when it investigated Best from the south, but the blown bridge over the Wilhelmina Canal prevented Weatherby from assisting B Sqn and C Sqn in their costly battle. The fighting at Best drew Allied forces to the west at a critical time, for that same afternoon Panzer-Brigade 107 closed in on the corridor from the east without meeting any opposition.

Early on 19 September the leading elements of Panzer-Brigade 107 left their unloading areas in Venlo and Roermond and headed west under the cover of a foggy morning. In Helmond they picked up I. Bataillon/Fallschirmjäger Ersatz- und Ausbildungs-Regiment Greve under command of Hauptmann Karl Vosshage. This replacement unit of German 'paratroopers' was scraped together from Luftwaffe ground personnel and only a small core of around 30 per cent had actually received parachute training. The battalion fielded four rifle companies with plenty of automatic small arms but lacked heavy weapons.

OPPOSITE
As the bulk of 15/19 Hussars assisted the US 101st Airborne Division on the western flank around Best on 19 September, Panzer-Brigade 107 advanced from the east but found its freedom of manoeuvre restricted by the Dommel River and Wilhelmina Canal.

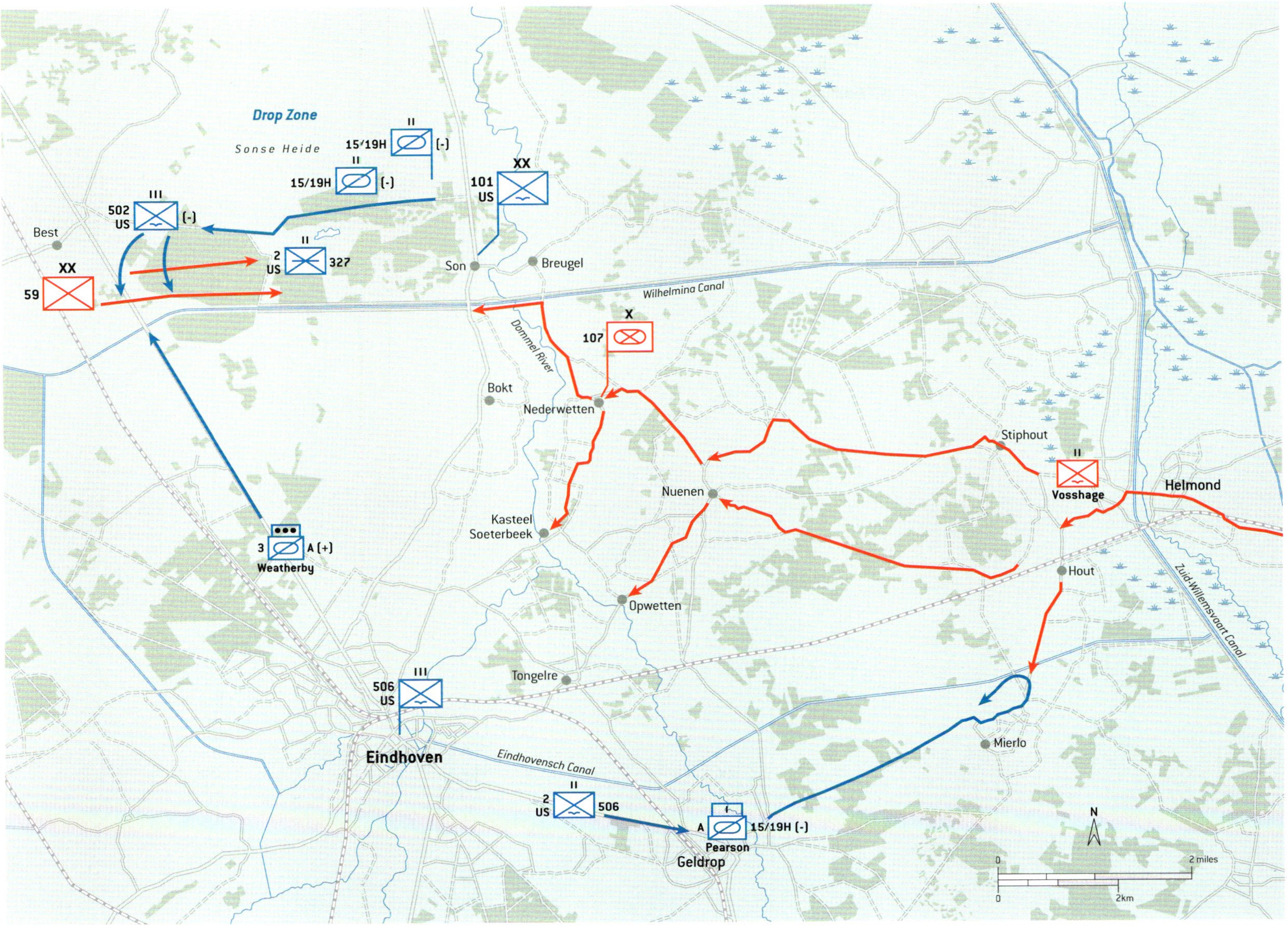

Drop Zone
Sonse Heide
15/19H
(-)
II
15/19H
(-)
II
XX
101
US
III
502
US
(-)
Best
II
2
US
327
XX
59
Son
Breugel
Wilhelmina Canal
Dommel River
X
107
Bokt
Nederwetten
Stiphout
II
Vosshage
Helmond
Nuenen
Kasteel
Soeterbeek
3
A (+)
Weatherby
Hout
Opwetten
Zuid-Willemsvaart Canal
Tongelre
III
506
US
Mierlo
Eindhoven
Eindhovensch Canal
II
2
US
506
A
15/19H (-)
Pearson
Geldrop
N
0
2 miles
0
2km

The original mission of Panzer-Brigade 107 called for a quick march through German-held Eindhoven to take up a blocking position south of the city, but now that Eindhoven had been taken by American paratroopers and British armour was surging through it, the German focus had shifted north to Son. Between Helmond and Son lay an area of flat farmland, small woods and villages that was boxed in by several waterways. The Wilhelmina Canal to the north, Zuid-Willemsvaart Canal to the east, Eindhovensch Canal to the south and Dommel River to the west severely restricted any form of mechanized manoeuvre. The area was also hostile as far as the Germans knew. Vast airborne landings, a breakthrough by the Guards Armoured Division, prowling Allied aircraft overhead and Dutch resistance activity in the rear made for an uneasy situation, especially for a unit that had only just arrived in the theatre.

With the scouts in the lead, Panzer-Brigade 107 probed its way into the area west of Helmond. By the late afternoon it had established a firm base in the crossroads village of Nuenen and advanced further west into Nederwetten where Major Maltzahn set up his command post. The brigade was a stone's throw away from the vital Allied supply line, but the winding Dommel River prevented a direct strike. The Dommel ran parallel to the main road from the northern outskirts of Eindhoven to its intersection with the Wilhelmina Canal at Son, effectively shielding the road from the east. German scouts probed the minor road that led south out of Nederwetten to Eindhoven but ran into a rickety bridge over the Dommel at Soeterbeek and a local who emphatically told them that the structure could not support heavy traffic. No other bridge spanned the Dommel, except for a small footbridge at the Hooidonk watermill, until the intersection with the Wilhelmina Canal at Son where a sturdy culvert provided the only passage to the west. A flanking move to the north had been made impossible by the German decision preventively to blow all minor bridges over the Wilhelmina Canal in the days preceding Operation *Market Garden*, leaving Panzer-Brigade 107 with no choice but to use the culvert. Ordering an attack in column formation over a raised canal embankment that was barely wide enough for a single Panther was a risky move, but with the day almost over Maltzahn was anxious to launch an attack while he still had the element of surprise.

The arrival of German tanks in Helmond had been passed on to the Allies by the local resistance network, but the overstretched 101st Airborne Division still had its attention fixed to the west. The 2d Battalion of the 506th PIR had set out from Eindhoven to Helmond earlier in the afternoon, but the footsore American paratroopers quickly marched back when they spotted German armour outside Helmond. Major General Taylor was still waiting for confirmation when tank shells blasted the top floor of his command post in Son. A platoon of Panthers with supporting infantry had made it over the culvert and opened fire as the tanks slowly advanced along the narrow southern canal bank. A supply lorry from the Guards Armoured Division's Q Bty, 21 AT Regt RA, was on its way to join the guns near Nijmegen and crossed the Son Bailey bridge at an unfortunate time. The fully laden lorry was struck by a shell from one of the Panthers and burst into flames.

Headquarters personnel, airborne engineers, glider pilots and lorry drivers scrambled to organize a defence. Their small-arms fire kept the German infantry at bay, but bazooka anti-tank rocket launchers alone failed to stop the Panthers. Thankfully the division's heavy weapons had arrived by glider just hours earlier and a

PANTHER GUNSIGHT

The Panther Ausf G was equipped with the dual-magnification TZF 12a sighting telescope. The low-power setting offered 2.5× magnification with a fairly wide field of view of 28 degrees for target acquisition. Once the target was found, the gunner switched to a high-power setting that offered 5x magnification with a narrower field of view of 14 degrees for precise aiming at longer ranges.

The graticule consisted of a hollow triangle flanked by rows of smaller triangles that served as 'aim-off' markers for holding lead on moving targets. Additionally, the size of a target in relation to the triangles gave a rough indication of the distance, provided the dimensions of the target were known. Range settings for all available ammunition types were arranged in a rotating circular scale. The gunner aligned the fixed pointer at the top of the sight with the desired range for the appropriate ammunition type. One half of the circle was a range scale for the coaxial MG 34 and the Sprgr 42 HE shell, the other half featured range scales for the Pzgr 39/42 APCBC and Pzgr 40/42 APCR high-velocity ammunition. Adjusting the range setting moved the central graticule up or down. Once the sight was dialled in, the gunner used the point of the large triangle as an aiming mark.

towed gun from the 81st Airborne Antiaircraft Battalion was pointed to a firing position by Taylor, who was personally leading the defence. Its crew deployed the 57mm piece just in time to catch the lead tank in the right flank as it approached the southern end of the bridge. The stricken Panther tried to reverse but concentrated fire from the anti-tank gun and bazookas convinced the crew that bailing out was their best option. Shortly afterwards a penetrating hit struck ammunition and the Panther's turret was ripped apart by the ensuing blast. Panzer-Brigade 107 had lost its first tank and with it the element of surprise.

It was now clear to the Germans that their options for mechanized manoeuvre were exhausted. As neither the Dommel nor the Wilhelmina Canal offered any alternative crossing points for Panthers besides the exposed southern embankment, there was no other choice than to switch their tactics around. The burden of the next attack would fall on the infantry while the Panthers provided fire support. By positioning the tanks close to the Wilhelmina Canal they could fire west over the Dommel and onto the Allied supply line while the high canal embankment simultaneously shielded them from the anti-tank guns to their north. The tanks would be reduced to the role of static fire support, but at least they would have their flanks covered and a decent field of fire to their front. The most difficult mission was given to Hauptmann Vosshage and his poorly trained light-infantry battalion. It was ordered to cross the Dommel using the footbridge at the Hooidonk watermill during the night and then push into Son at daybreak under the covering fire of the Panthers.

As Major Maltzahn was issuing his attack orders from the pub in Nederwetten, Major General Taylor was gathering forces to bolster his defence. The 81st Airborne Antiaircraft Battalion was ordered to wheel more 57mm guns out of the gliders and into positions around Son. Four heavier 3in guns mounted in M10 self-propelled guns were provided by J Tp, 198 Bty, 73 AT Regt RA. This British unit had been escorting the large supply column that was cut by the German attack and J Tp remained in Son to keep the Panthers at bay until the convoy had passed. On the landing fields north-west of Son, 20 75mm pack howitzers from the airborne artillery were pushed into battery positions next to their gliders. Additional indirect fire was provided by the eight Sexton self-propelled artillery vehicles of 341 Bty RA. Infantrymen from the 1st Battalion of the 327th Glider Infantry Regiment (GIR) were marched straight out of their gliders and into Son. The unit was understrength as many gliders had missed the landing zone, but what was left of Co. A dug in west of the main road while the remains of Co. C took the eastern side. The bulk of 1/506th PIR came marching up the road from Eindhoven and took up defensive positions behind the canal to the east of Son. Lastly, Taylor turned his attention to 15/19 Hussars. He had called for the regiment's help as soon as the German tanks appeared outside his command post, but B Sqn and C Sqn had been fully committed to the heavy fighting near Best. Now that the immediate danger had passed, the regiment regrouped in its leaguer just north-west of Son for maintenance and resupply.

Meanwhile in the south, A Sqn's two task forces did not have the luxury of a safe leaguer or even resupply. They had returned from their patrols that evening only to find Eindhoven in a state of panic. News of the German tank attack was exaggerated by wild rumours that the Bailey bridge at Son had been destroyed and German armour

A Panther of Panzer-Brigade 107 has met its end in a Dutch field. The wreck had largely been stripped for scrap metal by the time this photograph was taken. The *Schürzen* side skirts were usually the first parts to be carried off by locals, right after Allied troops had scrounged for souvenirs. (RHC Eindhoven 21015/0214902-002)

was closing in on the city. Colonel Robert F. Sink of the 506th PIR quickly ordered A Sqn into blocking positions at the roads leading into Eindhoven. Later that evening, 44 RTR arrived and added its Shermans to the city's hasty defences. Just when Eindhoven was choked with Allied forces and Dutch civilians, the German Luftwaffe carried out a bombing raid on the city centre. One bomb landed near A Sqn's supply echelon as it was forming up to resupply the tanks. A lorry carrying ammunition was hit and set off a chain reaction that ignited two petrol tankers, destroyed a supply lorry and also the fitters' half-track.

That night the fires in Eindhoven lit up the southern horizon as both sides made their final preparations for next day's battle. One American gliderman was digging his foxhole on the outskirts of Son when he heard the distant rumbling of Panther tanks prowling in the dark. Just a few hundred metres south at the watermill, a farmer was kept awake by hobnailed boots marching cautiously over the narrow footbridge. The seemingly endless flow of Allied *matériel* continued steadily on its way north, the sleep-deprived lorry drivers unaware of the battle being prepared around them. In their leaguer outside Son, troop leaders and squadron commanders were taking stock of their remaining tanks as tired crews performed maintenance on weary machines. It had been exactly one month since 15/19 Hussars' first encounter with a Panther outside Argentan, during which time the regiment had learned a lot.

THE BATTLE FOR SON, 20 SEPTEMBER 1944

A sharp firefight erupted in the early morning mist as one of Co. C's outposts was fighting for its life. The crackling of automatic small-arms fire reached a crescendo, then died down as the position was overrun. The outpost had given valuable early warning to the rest of the company that held a thin defensive line south of Son, stretching from the large solitary windmill that stood by the main road down to the banks of the Dommel River. The glider 'company' was reduced to a single rifle platoon and its supporting weapons after a chaotic flight over the Channel, so Captain Walter L. Miller had to make the most of his available machine guns to cover the open fields to his south. Almost as an afterthought a string of anti-tank mines was placed along the front by airborne engineers.

The last stand of its outpost had put Co. C on full alert. When the first *Fallschirmjäger* appeared out of the mist, they were met by grazing machine-gun fire that quickly drove them out of the open fields and into shallow ditches that led to the American lines. Captain Miller guided his riflemen into blocking positions and the first German attack was quickly brought to a standstill by massed American rifle fire.

The delicate balance swung around as the early morning mist dissipated. A short distance to the east, with the rising sun at their backs, five Panthers began zeroing in on muzzle flashes in the twilight. The tanks were nestled into the corner between the Dommel and the Wilhelmina Canal from where they brought heavy suppressing fire to bear on Co. C, opening the way for another push by the German infantry. A platoon of engineers and some headquarters men bravely joined the defence but could not prevent the American line from buckling under the pressure. The dawn also exposed British traffic on the road, turning it into a shooting gallery for the German tanks. A fuel lorry took a direct hit and exploded in a great fireball, blanketing the area in thick black smoke. Further south German infantry was surging across the Dommel into the undefended stretch between Eindhoven and Son, taking up positions in farms and orchards and shooting more British lorries off the road.

Lieutenant-Colonel A.D. Taylor of 15/19 Hussars had meanwhile returned to Son after his perilous reconnaissance mission. He quickly ordered Major the Lord Rathdonnell to take B Sqn south of the canal to stabilize the crumbling front line and keep the German infantry away from the bridge. Turning to Major G. Courage of C Sqn, Taylor ordered him to send one of his troops east to try to get an angle on the German flank from across the canal. B Sqn set out across the Bailey bridge around 0700hrs. Rathdonnell's force had been the hardest hit by a month of combat and was reduced to just eight operational tanks organized around 1 and 3 Tp. Lieutenant Frazer led 1 Tp after the loss of Lieutenant Sharpe to the Panther at Argentan, while 3 Tp under Lieutenant M. Jennings is likely to have included a Challenger commanded by Corporal S. Potter.

The eight tanks fanned out beyond the houses and gardens that lined the main road south of Son, weaving past abandoned or destroyed lorries and avoiding ditches filled with survivors from the convoy. Ahead of them they could see groups of German infantrymen dashing and crawling through the fields and ditches towards Co. C's hard-pressed position. The concentrated firepower of B Sqn's eight tanks brought the German advance to a dead stop. From further in the rear artillery shells whistled over the roofs of Son and crashed down on the pinned German troops. Their morale broke in the face of such overwhelming firepower and Rathdonnell ordered his squadron to pursue and sweep the road clear. All appeared well as Rathdonnell and his second-in-command, Captain R.H.W. Ellis, approached the windmill that stood beside the main road just south of Son, but they could not know that they had passed Co. C's line and were driving towards the unmarked minefield. Captain Miller, despite a wound in his leg, ran up to warn them.

During the confusion a Panther crew's attention was drawn to the activity at the windmill. Upon seeing the boxy shapes of the two Cromwells, the commander ordered an armour-piercing round to be loaded as he guided the gunner's aim past bushes and buildings towards the distant targets. Over at the windmill, Captain Miller was just climbing onto Rathdonnell's tank when an incoming high-velocity round scraped across the top of the turret in a shower of sparks. The crew quickly bailed out as the Panther's gunner set his sight onto the second-in-command's Cromwell. This time the Panther struck the bulky barrel of the close-support Cromwell's 95mm howitzer, tearing out a large chunk but leaving the crew unharmed. The driver reversed and nearly buried an American infantryman in his foxhole before Captain Miller once again intervened and got the tank moving in a safe direction.

The five Panthers beyond the Dommel River remained elusive targets despite their frequent firing. Tree branches were draped over their three-colour camouflage paint and the commanders had picked their positions well. As far as B Sqn could tell, the Panthers were practically 'hull down' from a westerly direction. A tank's survival relies as much on its mobility as on its armour or camouflage, however, and the Panthers were rooted to their position by the terrain and the mission. The longer they remained in place, the heavier the return fire became. Airborne gunners were bravely banging away with their 57mm pieces and some paratroopers were ambitiously launching bazooka rockets across the canal. The M10s of J Tp spotted two distant Panthers and arced some shots their way without observing a hit. In the south, Shermans and Fireflies from C Sqn, 44 RTR, had set out from Eindhoven in the direction of Son and fired at suspicious shapes across the Dommel. More Shermans briefly got involved as a column of the Sherwood Rangers Yeomanry raced through the battle on its way to Nijmegen.

In the thunderous exchange of fire one Panther suffered a fatal hit from a high-velocity gun. Major Courage of C Squadron writes in his 1949 history of the 15/19 Hussars that Major M.S. Balmain, the regiment's second-in-command, had directed a '17-pr SP gun' to fire at a presumed Panther and that this quick intervention knocked out the German tank that was shooting at the B Sqn Cromwells near the windmill. His description leaves the exact mount of the 17-pdr a mystery, although a Challenger is a likely candidate and may have become confused with the M10s of J Tp during the chaos of battle and the subsequent retelling. Regardless of its origin, the 17-pdr shot not only destroyed a Panther but also broke the German stranglehold on the Allied lifeline as the four remaining Panthers threw up a smokescreen and began their retreat.

As the battle was raging south of the canal, Lieutenant M. Mather's 4 Tp, C Sqn, had been prowling the northern bank in search of the German flank. Leading the way were two inconspicuous scout cars from the Reconnaissance Squadron led by Lieutenant K.F. Butler and Sergeant A. Spanton. They crossed the Dommel between

OVERLEAF
'Hell's Highway' has been held by the combined efforts of the British 15/19 Hussars and US 327th Glider Infantry Regiment. Smoke rises in the distance from a knocked-out Panther. Four more will be destroyed by 15/19 Hussars before the day is over and Panzer-Brigade 107 abandons its attack on Son.

13

Unlike most Panthers knocked-out during the fighting around Son, this one has not had its layer of *Zimmerit* anti-magnetic coating fully burned away by an internal ammunition fire. Some foliage still clings to the wreck. Most vehicles of Panzer-Brigade 107 were thoroughly camouflaged with local flora to hide them from Allied air power. (RHC Eindhoven 20210/0110141)

Son and Breugel, then swung right in the latter village and followed the narrow road south to where the blown secondary bridge over the Wilhelmina Canal once provided passage to Nederwetten. Some skirmishing was going on between American paratroopers and German snipers across the canal, but the Panthers were perfectly 'turret down' behind the high embankment and out of reach of 4 Tp's guns. Butler and Spanton stalked the German tanks from the northern bank, perhaps using the perch provided by the house near the blown bridge to peek over the embankment. Mather's troop kept a safe distance, likely staying on the firm brick road as the surrounding fields were soft and lined with ditches.

The Panthers remained tucked into their corner until one of them was knocked out in the duel across the Dommel and the others decided to pull back. One by one they launched smoke grenades to their west, turned around and headed for the dirt road that led back to Nederwetten. This manoeuvre briefly brought them out of cover as the ground around this road gently rises up to the level of the embankment. Likewise on the northern bank, the gentle increase in elevation provided a perfect ramp for a British tank to move into a firing position. The scouts notified 4 Tp of the opportunity and its Challenger under Corporal R. Isaacs answered the call. The driver crept the machine forward until the gunner's sight had cleared the top of the embankment. In the open field just south of the canal, a Panther was dashing from right to left. The Challenger's gunner laid the 17-pdr gun squarely on the target and fired. At a mere 400m the AP shot reached the Panther in the blink of an eye. It effortlessly penetrated

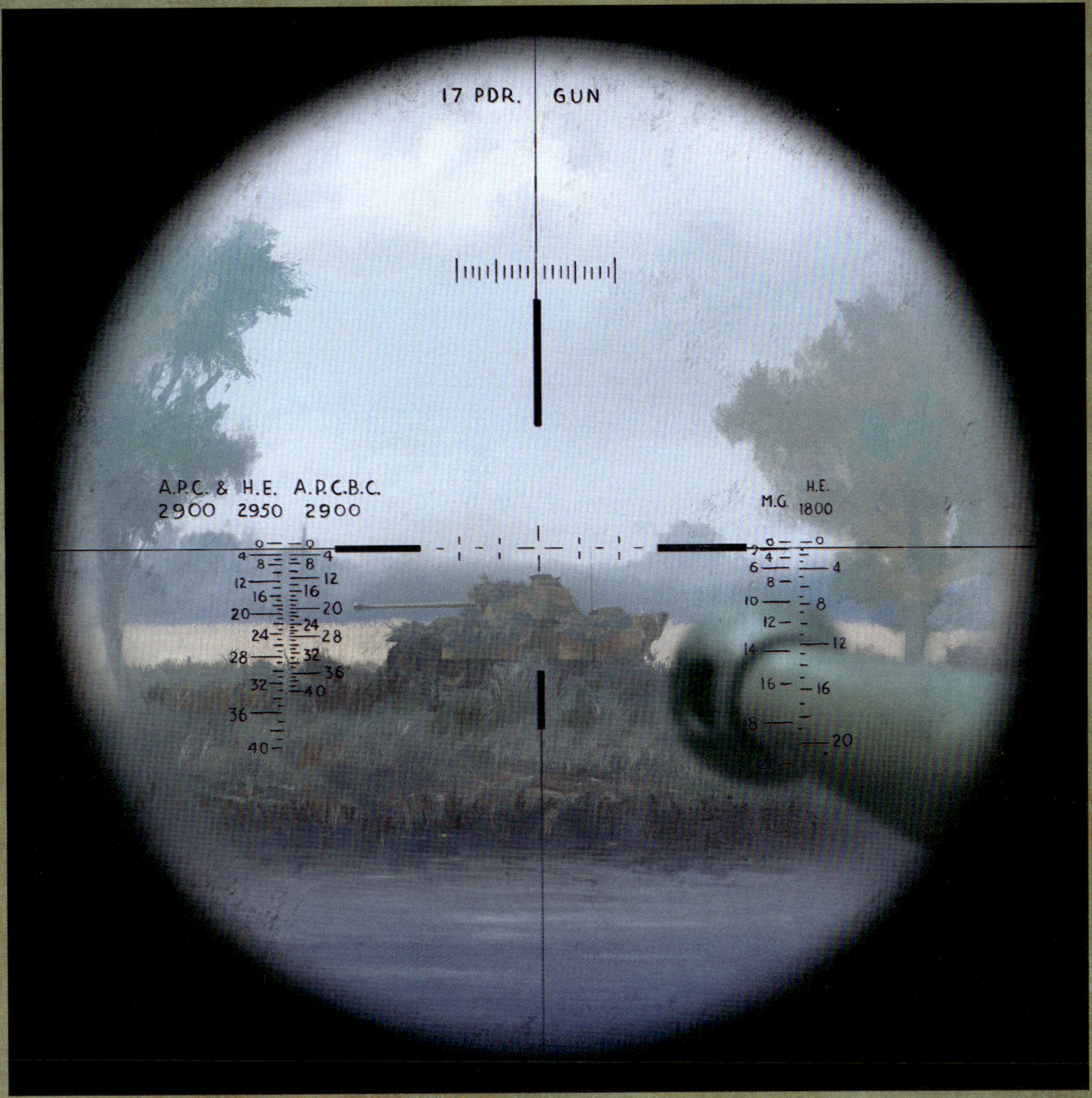

A30 CHALLENGER GUNSIGHT

Most Challengers were equipped with the No. 43 ×3 ML Mk III sighting telescope. Only the first 23 Challengers made use of the Mk I version of the sight and the interim Mk II was never installed. The 'M' in 'ML' indicated that the scopes had a moving graticule that could be adjusted for elevation and deflection. The 'L' indicated that the graticule could be illuminated in red with adjustable brightness.

The Mk III version mainly updated the range scales to include the flat trajectory of the aerodynamic APCBC shot and the curved trajectory of the reduced-charge HE shell, although the latter was not used by the Challenger. There was no range scale for the high-velocity APDS shot, which further reduced the practical accuracy of this temperamental ammunition type. The Mk III sight also added a scale for easier deflection adjustment, although this feature had limited utility. An open cross served as the aiming mark after earlier sights with solid crosshairs were criticized for obscuring the target at long range. The central aiming mark was flanked by 'aim-off' lines that were used for holding lead on moving targets. The scopes provided 3× magnification with a field of view of 13 degrees. An alternative 6× eyepiece was developed, but proved unpopular with gunners due to its narrower field of view and associated eyestrain.

This crew of C Sqn's 4 Tp went to great lengths to camouflage the Challenger's conspicuous turret and long 17-pdr gun with foliage. Concealment was especially important for the Challenger as it had a higher profile than the Cromwells it accompanied and thus stood out as a priority target. (Tank Museum 0037-G5)

the tank's thin side plate, entered the fighting compartment in a spray of splinters that struck crew and ammunition, then punched through the other side with excess energy. The Panther rolled to a standstill just short of the road to Nederwetten and started to burn. Panzer-Abteilung 2107 recorded its second tank loss to *'feind-Pak'* (enemy anti-tank guns) and blamed the failure of the attack on insurmountable terrain obstacles and overwhelming Allied firepower.

As morning turned to noon Panzer-Brigade 107 switched to a defensive footing. With the Panthers gone, the six remaining tanks of B Sqn were free to sweep the main road clear of lingering German infantry in cooperation with the Shermans of 44 RTR. This was still dangerous work as Sergeant A. Yeomans was wounded in the head by small-arms fire while commanding his tank from an open hatch. Wrecked vehicles were pushed off the road and the flow of traffic resumed as if nothing had happened. A more thorough clearing of the marshy Dommel riverbank had to wait until 1145hrs while the American glidermen reorganized themselves into a wide sweep line from the road to the river. B Sqn supported their advance by firing whole belts of machine-gun ammunition into suspected enemy positions. Combing out the ditches, bushes and orchards revealed over 50 German dead and brought in 185 prisoners including the commander, Hauptmann Vosshage.

WEATHERBY STRIKES BACK, 20 SEPTEMBER 1944

By the end of the morning the threat to Son had passed and B Sqn and C Sqn could rest easy knowing they had played their part. Meanwhile in Eindhoven, the shock from the previous night's bombardment had turned into a determination to strike back at the Germans. Colonel Sink was in command of a sizeable British armoured force and would not have them sit idly on the city outskirts. Pearson Force was ordered east again to Geldrop but made no contact with the enemy. To its north, B Sqn,44 RTR, carried Co. E, 506th PIR, to the village of Nuenen where they ran into concealed Panthers and a counter-attack by German infantry. A second attack on the village by

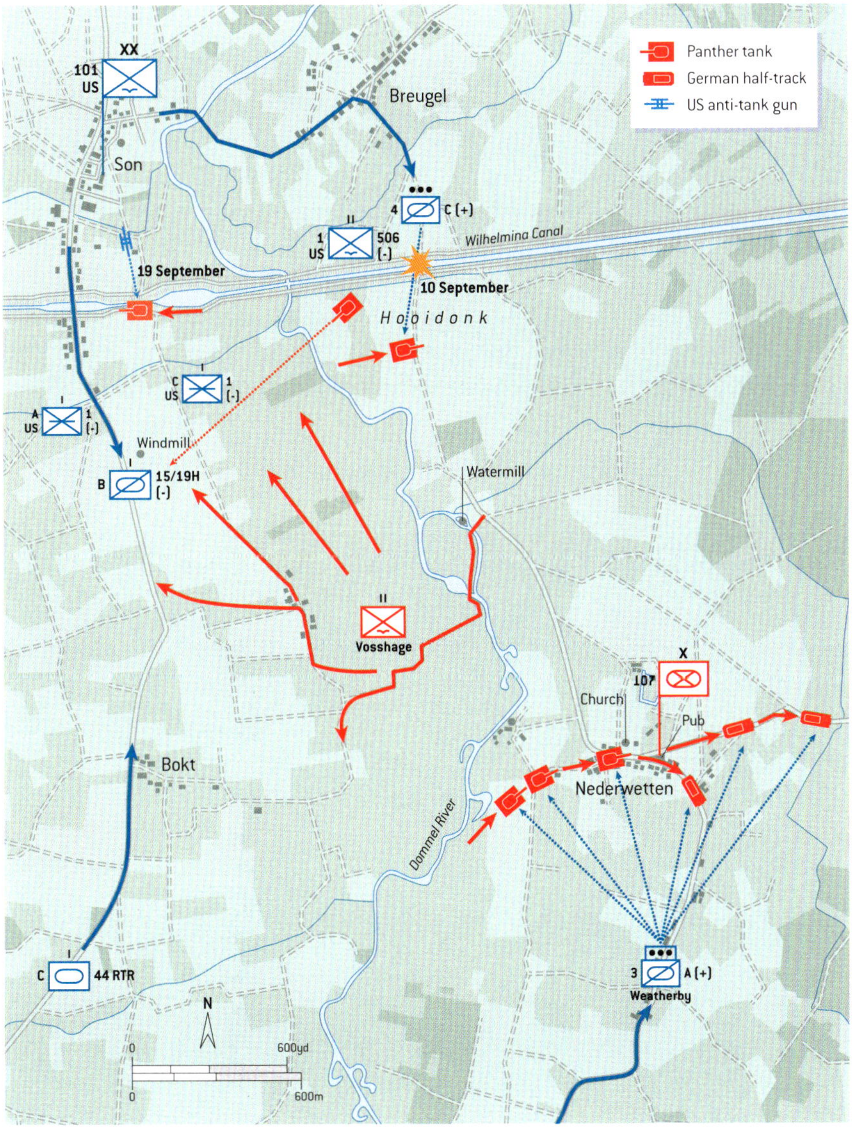

Having lost the element of surprise the previous evening, Panzer-Brigade 107 committed its Panthers to a static fire support role on 20 September. Superior Allied firepower smashed the German infantry west of the Dommel River and the retreating Panthers were picked off by flanking attacks of 15/19 Hussars.

A Sqn and Co. F was equally unsuccessful. To their west Weatherby Force had better luck. The small force consisted of Lieutenant C.C. Egerton's 3 Tp including a Challenger commanded by Sergeant Gadd, two scout cars from the Reconnaissance Squadron under Lieutenant B.W.B. Sparrow and Corporal Hunter and squads of American paratroopers from Co. A, 506th PIR. Captain Weatherby led his party from a close-support Cromwell.

Shortly after setting out in the morning the force found its way blocked by the same narrow bridge over the Dommel at Soeterbeek that had discouraged the German scouts the previous afternoon. Not long before Weatherby arrived a patrol from C Sqn, 44 RTR, had also inspected the crossing and driven off a picket of German infantry, but they too judged the bridge unsuited for tanks. Weatherby, however, was willing to take the risk if it meant surprising the Germans. The scout cars made it across without incident followed by the tanks. The bridge was so narrow that the guardrails were damaged by the tanks, but thankfully the Challenger was no wider than the Cromwells and it too made it over. Weatherby Force was on the loose behind enemy lines.

The scout cars probed their way north until they reached a string of roadside farms and orchards just south of Nederwetten. There Lieutenant Sparrow surprised a small group of Germans with a burst from his Bren. The American paratroopers rushed in and took three prisoners, clearing the way for the tanks to take up positions among the shaded farmyards. Lieutenant Egerton and his troop sergeant were observing to the north-west, keeping an eye on the outskirts of Nederwetten about 600m away. The third Cromwell and the Challenger were watching the east and the two scout cars had repositioned to cover the rear.

It was around 1300hrs when a cloud of dust, a puff of exhaust smoke or a glint of metal drew Lieutenant Egerton's gaze to a distant field just west of Nederwetten. Through his binoculars he saw a Panther moving north-east and exposing its right

A squadron's triad of firepower on display. A close-support Cromwell with its 95mm howitzer can be seen at the front. The Challengers, easily recognizable by their tall turrets, are the squadron's 'hole punchers' mounting 17-pdr guns. The bulk of the tanks are regular Cromwells equipped with the 75mm dual-purpose gun. (British Official Photograph/FPG/Archive Photos/Getty Images)

One Panther was destroyed within sight of the Nederwetten pub where Panzer-Brigade 107 had its headquarters. Given its location, this is most likely the Panther engaged by Sergeant Nesbitt of Lieutenant Egerton's troop. The Hussars did not claim to have destroyed this Panther, so it may have been immobilized and later scuttled by the retreating Germans. (RHC Eindhoven 20096/0064507)

flank to the British tanks. Egerton had no time to whistle up his Challenger nor the need. His gunner found the target, quickly adjusted for range and lead and then sent a shot curving over the fields and into the thin side of the Panther. As Egerton focused on the burning wreck, Sergeant Nesbitt, Egerton's troop sergeant, spotted another Panther moving into the village. Nesbitt's gunner fired off a hasty shot that disappeared among the houses along with the enemy tank. The Panther likely came to a standstill in the village with a severed right track where it was later blown up by the retreating Germans. A tense quiet returned to the area that only lasted briefly. Shortly before 1400hrs, Egerton again saw movement where he had knocked out his first tank as another Panther made a dash for Nederwetten. His gunner already knew the correct range and lead and scored another broadside hit with his first round. Three more shots were put into the Panther until its ammunition caught fire and it finally 'brewed up'.

Captain Weatherby had led his force into a bountiful cut-off position and had already inflicted more tank losses than B Sqn and C Sqn combined. Hearing of his success, Major Pearson reinforced Weatherby with 2 Tp, A Sqn, and a 1 Royal Dragoons patrol. The fast cruiser tanks and armoured cars arrived just in time to engage a group of German half-tracks that was retreating through Nederwetten. Two were hit on the eastern road; a third took a wrong turn in the village and was struck as it rounded the corner where the British tanks stood.

By now the Germans were putting pressure on Weatherby Force to secure their line of retreat. Small-arms fire snapped through the orchards and an unidentified high-velocity gun began firing down the road. At 1540hrs Weatherby decided that the position had served its purpose and he fell back a short distance. The Germans did not pursue and around 1700hrs Weatherby received orders to return to Eindhoven. The young captain received the Military Cross for the skilful handling of his small force, which had not lost a single man or machine in the fight.

AFTERMATH AND ANALYSIS

A BATTLE LOST AND WON

By nightfall on 20 September both sides had disengaged. B Sqn and C Sqn stood vigilant in their fighting positions on the flanks of Son while Captain Weatherby and Major Pearson had pulled back their forces to the outskirts of Eindhoven for the night. Panzer-Brigade 107 shortened its overextended lines by giving up Nederwetten, Nuenen and Mierlo to establish a more defensible bridgehead over the Zuid-Willemsvaart Canal west of Helmond.

Much to the relief of 15/19 Hussars its parent formation, 11th Armoured Division, finally made headway the next day and came surging up the eastern flank as the spearhead of VIII Corps. It swept past Eindhoven and pushed into the pocket of Panzers by the afternoon of 21 September. More Panthers succumbed to the guns of Shermans as Panzer-Brigade 107 fought a rearguard action back to Helmond. By evening the brigade had fully retreated across the Zuid-Willemsvaart Canal. With the eastern flank secure, 15/19 Hussars had completed its mission to support the 101st Airborne Division and rejoined 11th Armoured Division that same day.

The surprise attack of the Panthers had caused a brief panic on 19 September when they first appeared so close to the Allied corridor, but by the 20th their threat had largely been contained. Both sides could look at a map and see that there was no way

The Panther was ideally suited for long-range engagements, but the dense and fragmented terrain commonly encountered in Western Europe funnelled tanks into predictable approaches that exposed their flanks to close-range ambushes. If caught in the flank, the Panther's relatively thinly armoured sides could be pierced by most Allied guns. (michael cremin/Alamy Stock Photo)

for Panthers to get onto the Allied corridor except via the narrow culvert – and this constricted approach could be denied by light airborne anti-tank weapons, as had been demonstrated on the evening of the 19th. By 20 September the Germans were facing bolstered defences backed by the equivalent of two tank battalions and by the 21st they had an armoured division pushing into their flank.

From the moment it had set out from Helmond on 19 September, Panzer-Brigade 107 was stretched beyond its intended role. It was advancing into an unfamiliar area without a clear picture of the enemy, the terrain or friendly forces. It had to dilute its strength to cover a wide southern flank and could not mass at a decisive point; neither could it manoeuvre around terrain obstacles or enemy strongpoints. It had no bridging equipment, no artillery, poor reconnaissance assets and an inadequate supply echelon that was still being unloaded at distant railheads. What it did have were fuel-hungry and maintenance-heavy Panther tanks that were stuck behind a minor river.

Yet the brigade's fire did cut the road to Arnhem on two occasions. Traffic came to a standstill on the evening of 19 September as Panthers rolled up to the Son Bailey bridge while the Luftwaffe bombed Eindhoven and again on the morning of the 20th when the Panthers and *Fallschirmjäger* swept the road south of Son with their fire. These were costly delays at a time when the Guards Armoured Division found its advance halted at Nijmegen by the failure of the 82d Airborne Division to capture the Waal bridge in time.

Repulsing Panzer-Brigade 107 at Son offered only a temporary reprieve. By 22 September the Panthers had moved slightly north and were lunging at the corridor again between Veghel and Uden where it was still narrow and its flanks unguarded. This time there was no river to keep the Germans back and they physically occupied a stretch of road for 24 hours until they were driven off. It was the last time Panzer-Brigade 107 threatened the corridor, but on the 24th a German force including *Jagdpanther* tank destroyers severed it again from the west at the hamlet of Koevering and kept it occupied for nearly two days. The continued assaults on the corridor, spearheaded by Panzer-Brigade 107, helped bring Operation *Market Garden* to a standstill short of its final objective.

AFTERMATH

In the closing days of *Market Garden*, 11th Armoured Division chased Panzer-Brigade 107 to the Peel marshes west of the Maas where the Germans made a stand. From late September to early November the brigade formed the armoured backbone

A Panther dwarfs a PzKpfw IV medium tank on its way to the front. While the PzKpfw IV was quickly upgraded with improved protection and firepower to remain competitive, it did not offer the leap in quality that German tankers demanded. Nevertheless it soldiered on until the end of the war as Panther production remained insufficient to replace it fully. (michael cremin/Alamy Stock Photo)

Field Marshal Montgomery and other dignitaries inspect Challengers and Cromwells of 8 King's Royal Irish Hussars from a half-track at the British victory parade in Berlin, 21 July 1945. Montgomery had hoped that the Challenger could fully replace the Cromwell, but was disappointed to learn that it was merely a stopgap. (The Print Collector/ Getty Images)

of the beleaguered salient. Only around ten Panthers were operational on any given day, but as a mobile reserve they were in their element. From concealed positions in woods and villages the Panthers inflicted disproportionate losses on roadbound Allied armour. Panzer-Brigade 107 had a few more encounters with 15/19 Hussars before the brigade was pulled out in early November to rejoin the ranks of the revived 25. Panzergrenadier-Division.

Around this time 15/19 Hussars received its first Sherman Firefly as Challenger production was not keeping up with losses. The tankers preferred the fast Cromwell and its derivatives over the American Sherman and found it to be an awkward addition to a troop. Another stopgap was received in March 1945 in the form of the Comet. This last addition to the British cruiser tank family was borne out of the disappointment in the Challenger, in particular its high profile and reduced armour. Instead the Comet made a questionable concession in firepower by mounting a weaker gun in a cramped turret while its protection remained below par. The Comet

Challengers and a close-support Cromwell of 8 King's Royal Irish Hussars parade through Berlin on 21 July 1945. By this time both the Challenger and Cromwell were being replaced by the Comet, which in turn would gradually make way for the Centurion as the backbone of the post-war Royal Armoured Corps. (Tank Museum TM 10912-065)

was nevertheless popular with 15/19 Hussars and the rest of 11th Armoured Division during the final push into Germany. It replaced both the Cromwell and the Challenger, putting an end to the divide between regular cruiser tanks and specialist 'hole punchers'.

The Challenger quickly disappeared from service, although a self-propelled gun variant was used by the Royal Artillery in the post-war years. The SP2 Avenger self-propelled gun mainly improved the Challenger's high profile by reducing the hull height and mounting a more space-efficient 17-pdr gun and traverse mechanism in a thinly armoured and open-topped turret without a coaxial machine gun.

TANK VS TANK COMBAT

Panzer-Brigade 107 lost five Panther tanks on 20 September. Only one of these was claimed by a Challenger, three others were accounted for by Cromwells and one fell to a mysterious '17-pr SP gun' that may have been a Challenger of B Sqn. In return the Panthers knocked out two Shermans of 44 RTR at Nuenen and damaged two Cromwells of 15/19 Hussars at the Son windmill. Other vehicular losses on that day

The weakest part of the Panther's frontal armour was the turret. Here a shot has penetrated the turret front plate. While this 100mm plate was one of the thickest pieces of armour on the Panther, its near-vertical arrangement made it vulnerable to some of the more powerful Allied guns. (Imwar/Alamy Stock Photo)

included a number of German half-tracks and British lorries. More shots were undoubtedly fired at distant or speculative targets by both sides without concrete results that made it into the historical record.

The day's fighting was typical of how 'tank battles' were usually waged in North-West Europe. There were tanks and they fought in a battle, but the actual tank-on-tank combat was a scattered series of short and sharp troop-sized actions at fairly short ranges that resembled ambushes more than duels. Tanks that were stationary and concealed destroyed moving tanks that were unaware of the shooter's presence. A notable exception occurred during the duel across the Dommel when a Panther gained the initiative and the result was a messy exchange of fire from which the crewmen of two Cromwell tanks were lucky to walk away. At Nuenen the Panthers were on the defensive and successfully held back the attacks of two tank squadrons and paratrooper companies without suffering losses.

The Challenger's role was smaller than one would expect in a tank-on-tank battle. Weatherby Force did not require a 'hole puncher' for the flanks of Panthers and may have preferred to present the lower profile of its Cromwells to enemy observers instead of the Challenger's tall turret. C Sqn made the most deliberate use of a Challenger in its intended anti-tank role, but when a Panther finally presented itself, it offered an

The thick and angled glacis that shielded most of the Panther's frontal profile was a tough nut to crack, but by late 1944 improved ammunition fired from high-velocity guns was capable of penetrating the plate under certain conditions, aided by inconsistencies in the metallurgical quality caused by German resource shortages. (NARA)

The Challenger quickly disappeared from British service following the introduction of the Comet, but some of the liberated countries used Challengers in the post-war years while they were rebuilding their armed forces. This Challenger was acquired by the Royal Netherlands Army for study and training purposes until 1954 when the Centurion had just entered service. (NIMH 2155-045017)

easy broadside target at short range that a Cromwell could have handled. Only B Sqn was truly in need of a 'hole puncher' when it took fire at the Son windmill and the quick intervention of a 17-pdr gun provided the necessary firepower at the right time and place to make a difference.

The victory of 15/19 Hussars demonstrates the importance of basic tactical principles regardless of temporary technological advantages or disadvantages. While there was a real and sometimes dramatic asymmetry in the combat capabilities of World War II tanks, most tank-on-tank engagements were not decided by armour thickness or muzzle velocity alone, but by the proper application of tactical fundamentals such as mutual support, clever use of terrain and surprise fire from the flank.

A technological advantage in tank design can only be leveraged under the right tactical circumstances and these are mostly dictated by the terrain and the mission. Ultimately, the success of any tank, no matter how capable it appears on paper, depends on where, when and how it is used, who is using it, how it is sustained and how it is supported. Any tank will suffer if the crew is poorly trained, fuel is lacking, attacks are poorly planned, combined-arms support is absent and flanks are left open. Conversely, a tank that appears inferior on paper can still be very successful if manoeuvred into the right position at the right time with the proper support.

CONCLUSION

The Panther and Challenger were both conceived in late 1941 as a response to improvements in tank armour that had grown beyond the capabilities of existing tank armament to pierce. Beyond that conceptual origin the two tanks diverged due to fundamental differences in the strategic situation, tank procurement process and armoured doctrine of Britain and Germany.

A generational leap was demanded of the Panther to secure a qualitative edge for Germany's outnumbered armoured force and this was largely achieved in a remarkably short span of time. The Panther improved upon previous German tanks in nearly all respects and confronted the Allies with a formidable balance of mobility, protection

An up-armoured Challenger is displayed next to an Avenger. This self-propelled gun benefited from more space-efficient components that allowed it to fit the 17-pdr gun in a bespoke, open-topped turret on a modified Challenger hull with a lower overall profile. A limited production run of 80 Avengers commenced in 1945, too late to see action in World War II. (Tank Museum TM 1791-D2)

After a slow start, Panther production finally peaked in July 1944 before declining due to resource shortages and systematic aerial bombing of German industry. An Allied bombing raid crippled the MNH plant in Hannover in March 1945, shortly before US troops took the city. (NARA)

and firepower that was not truly matched until 1945. The price for rushing brand-new technology into front-line service was paid for in poor reliability, however. This was scant relief for Allied tankers that faced the Panther in combat, but it did cut into the operational readiness of a German tank fleet that was already grossly outnumbered.

The Challenger was designed as a stopgap measure and intended as a specialist 'hole puncher'. It had to match closely the specifications of the compact Cromwell while also mounting a heavy gun that was not yet optimized for tank use in a fully rotating turret. Despite these contradictory demands, the end result was a capable tank that inherited the excellent mobility and durability of the Cromwell, retained a similar level of protection and mounted Britain's best anti-tank gun in a quick-turning turret.

The Challenger did not fail as a battle tank when it was finally fielded, it failed as the quick stopgap that it was supposed to be. From the moment of its inception the Challenger was intended as the fastest way to field a 17-pdr gun on the existing Cromwell cruiser tank. In this it fundamentally failed because the Cromwell could not accommodate the only available 17-pdr turret without significant alterations to the hull. This defeated the purpose of a quick stopgap and ultimately doomed the Challenger to an awkward middle ground that had neither the ease of production of a true stopgap nor the leap in fighting quality of a completely new design such as the Panther.

The Challenger never escaped its reputation as an ungainly stopgap. The Comet was generally more popular on account of its sleeker profile and thicker armour. It mounted a weaker gun than the Challenger, but by the time it saw action in early 1945, few German tanks were left to oppose it. (Tank Museum TM 11536-006)

The Sherman Firefly was a better stopgap because it could fit the 17-pdr gun with only minor modifications. Despite the Firefly prototype being presented a full year later than the Challenger's, its relatively simple conversion process led to its rapid acceptance and a production run that overshadowed the Challenger tenfold. The Firefly was inferior to the Challenger in some respects, but it handsomely beat it in the one field that mattered most: availability.

Qualitatively, the Challenger featured an admirable combination of firepower, speed and durability, but it remained a Cromwell derivative and could not improve upon the shortcomings in protection and flotation that characterized Britain's cruiser tanks. The Challenger's belated up-armouring could not compensate for the inefficient vertical arrangement of its plates, while the shedding of tracks in muddy conditions tarnished its reputation for reliability. The envisaged role of the 17-pdr gun as a 'hole puncher' delayed the provision of effective HE and smoke shells while the sabot ammunition was still too rare and unreliable to live up to its full potential.

Actually matching the Panther in overall capability, instead of merely countering it with stopgap modifications, required breaking with doctrine and self-imposed limitations. In the latter half of 1943 the British made the leap, abandoning previously held width and weight restrictions to design a tank that was fit for future warfare. The resulting A41 Centurion main battle tank had a 17-pdr gun, Meteor engine and Merritt-Brown gearbox like the Challenger, but added a sloping glacis plate, space-efficient suspension, wide tracks and a sensible interior layout with ergonomic crew stations. The Centurion would have been a fine match for the Panther, but it arrived too late ever to face one in combat.

The Challenger did fight the Panther and won. It was not as numerous as the Firefly, as sleek as the Comet or as capable as the Centurion, but despite its flaws the Challenger ultimately fulfilled its purpose as an up-gunned Cromwell and was put in the right hands at the right place at the right time to make a difference.

BIBLIOGRAPHY

War diaries and award recommendations

Egerton, Lieutenant, MC recommendation (1944), The National Archives, WO 373/51/25

Kriegstagebuch der Panzer-Abteilung 2107 umbenannt in Panzer-Abteilung 5 (1944–1945), Central Archives of the Russian Ministry of Defence, 500-12483-91

Taylor, Lieutenant-Colonel, DSO recommendation (1944), The National Archives, WO 373/49/516

War Diary, 15/19 King's Royal Hussars (1944), The National Archives, WO 171/846

War Diary, 44 Royal Tank Regiment (1944), The National Archives, WO 171/873

War Diary, 73 Anti-Tank Regiment (1944), The National Archives, WO 171/924

War Diary, 198 Battery (1944), The National Archives, WO 171/942

Weatherby, Captain, MC recommendation (1944), The National Archives, WO 373/51/45

Manuals

AFV School, AFVP/GI/34, Challenger I Armament Training Pamphlet (1945)

Chief Inspector of Fighting Vehicles, Service Instruction Book for Challenger I, Chilwell Cat. No. 62/578 (1944), The Tank Museum, E2011-2569

D655/2, Panther Gerätebeschreibung und Bedienungsanweisung zum Turm (1944)

D655/5, Panther Handbuch für den Panzerfahrer (1944)

D655/27, Die Pantherfibel (1944)

Generalinspekteur der Panzertruppen, Richtlinien für Führung und Kampf der Panzer-Brigade (1944), Bundesarchiv RH 11-III/76

H.Dv.470/5e, Die Ausbildung am Panzerkampfwagen Panther (1943)

H.Dv.470/20, Panzerschießvorschrift für Panzerkampfwagen, Sturmgeschütze und Panzerspähwagen (1944)

H.Dv.481/55, Merkblatt für die Munition der 7,5cm Kampfwagenkanone 42 und 7,5cm Sturmkanone 42 (1943)

War Office, MTP No. 34, Royal Armoured Corps Weapon Training, Part 4: Tank Fire Tactics (1944)

War Office, MTP No. 41, The tactical handling of the Armoured Division and its components, Part 2: The Armoured Regiment (1943)
War Office, MTP No. 60, The tactical employment of Armoured Car and Reconnaissance Regiments, Part 1: General principles regarding the tactical employment of reconnaissance units (1943)

Studies and reports

A.30 – 'Challenger' (1947), The Tank Museum, E2011-2689
Military Operational Research Report No. 61, Study No. 11, Motion studies of German tanks (1947), The National Archives, WO 291/1003
Operations Research Office, ORO-T-117, Survey of Allied Tank Casualties in World War II (1951)
Preliminary Specification of A.30 Cruiser Tank, The Tank Museum, E2011-2686
Schacht, Gerhard, Die Kämpfe der Gruppe 'Walther' vom 13.9.1944 bis zum 12.10.1944 in Südholland (1954), Office of the Chief of Military History, MS P-188
Sixt, Friedrich, Die Kämpfe der Panzer-Brigade 107 im September und Oktober 1944 (1954), Office of the Chief of Military History, MS P-189

Books

Anderson, Thomas (2017). *Panther*. Munich: GeraMond Verlag.
Beale, Peter (2009). *Death by Design: British Tank Development in the Second World War*. Brimscombe: The History Press.
Bird, Lorrin R. & Livingston, Robert (2001). *World War II Ballistics: Armor and Gunnery*. Albany, NY: Overmatch Press.
Buckley, John (2004). *British Armour in the Normandy Campaign 1944*. London: Routledge.
Courage, G. (1949). *The History of 15/19 The King's Royal Hussars 1939–1945*. Aldershot: Gale & Polden.
Delaforce, Patrick (2010). *The Black Bull: From Normandy to the Baltic with the 11th Armoured Division*. Barnsley: Pen & Sword.
Didden, Jack & Swarts, Maarten (2018). *Kampfgruppe Walther and Panzerbrigade 107: A thorn in the side of Market Garden*. Drunen: Zwaardvisch Publishers.
Ellis, L.F. (1968). *Victory in the West, Vol. II: The Defeat of Germany*. Uckfield: HMSO.
Fletcher, David (2017). *British Battle Tanks: British-made Tanks of World War II*. Oxford: Osprey Publishing.
Hendrikx, Peter & de Trez, Michel (2012). *Orange is the Color of the Day: Pictorial History of the 101st Airborne Division during the Liberation of Holland*. Saint-Côme-du-Mont: D-Day Paratroopers Historical Center Publishing.
Jarymowycz, Roman (2009). *Tank Tactics: From Normandy to Lorraine*. Mechanicsburg, PA: Stackpole.
Jentz, Thomas, L. (1995). *Germany's Panther Tank: The Quest for Combat Supremacy*. Atglen, PA: Schiffer.
Knight, P.M. (2015). *A30 Challenger Tank: A Technical History*. Milton Keynes: Lulu.com.
Knight, P.M. (2016). *A34 Comet Tank: A Technical History*. Milton Keynes: Lulu.com.
Koskimaki, George E. (2007). *Hell's Highway: A Chronicle of the 101st Airborne Division in the Holland Campaign, September–November 1944*. Novato, CA: Presidio Press.
MacDonald, Charles, B. (1993). *The Siegfried Line Campaign*. Washington, DC: Center of Military History, US Army.
Margry, Karel (1982). *De bevrijding van Eindhoven*. Eindhoven: Lecturis.
Moore, Craig (2020). *How to Kill a Panther Tank: Unpublished Scientific Reports from the Second World War*. Stroud: Fonthill Media.
Perrett, Bryan (1981). *The PzKpfw V Panther*. Vanguard 21. London: Osprey Publishing.
Rapport, Leonard & Northwood, Jr, Arthur (2015). *Rendezvous with Destiny: A History of the 101st Airborne Division*. Old Saybrook, CT: Konecky & Konecky.
Schneider, Wolfgang (2020). *Panzer Tactics: German Small-Unit Armor Tactics in World War II*. Lanham, MD: Globe Pequot.
Spielberger, Walter J. (1993). *Panther and its Variants*. Atglen, PA: Schiffer.
Zaloga, Steven J. (2008). *Panther vs Sherman: Battle of the Bulge 1944*. Duel 13. Oxford: Osprey Publishing.

INDEX

Figures in **bold** refer to illustrations and tables.